LLOYD D. NEWELL AND ROBERT L. MILLET

WHEN *Ye* *Shall* RECEIVE THESE *Things*

DAILY REFLECTIONS ON THE BOOK OF MORMON

DESERET
BOOK

SALT LAKE CITY, UTAH

Library of Congress Cataloging-in-Publication Data

Newell, Lloyd D., 1956-
    When ye shall receive these things / Lloyd D. Newell, Robert L. Millet.
        p.   cm.
    ISBN 1-59038-162-9 (alk. paper)
    1. Book of Mormon—Devotional literature.   2. Devotional calendars—Church of Jesus Christ of Latter-day Saints. I. Millet, Robert L.   II. Title.
    BX8627.N44 2003
    289.3'22—dc22   2003017800

Printed in the United States of America   42316-0287R
Inland Press, Menomonee Falls, WI

10   9   8   7   6   5   4   3

To Nephi, Jacob, Mormon, and Moroni
the four principal writers of the Book of Mormon
whose words speak to us now as from the dust and whose
timely and timeless testimonies of Jesus Christ
shall yet shake the earth

PREFACE

The Prophet Joseph Smith taught that the Book of Mormon is the "keystone of our religion" (*Teachings*, 194). One of his successors, President Ezra Taft Benson, explained further that the book is the keystone of our witness of Christ, our doctrine, and our testimony (Conference Report, October 1986, 3–7). A lifting and liberating power seems to flow from its pages. That is surely what the Prophet Joseph had in mind when he observed that "a man would get nearer to God by abiding by its precepts, than by any other book" (*Teachings*, 194).

Christ-centered and gospel-centered, the Book of Mormon leads us to the Lord and motivates us to do good. God is the author of the book. Under the guidance of his Holy Spirit, men who knew the Lord and had partaken of his goodness and grace, men with seeric vision who saw our day, prepared their record with our obstacles and difficulties in mind. It speaks directly to us because it was written directly to us (Mormon 8:35; 9:30). Our challenge, therefore, is not just to read the Book of Mormon but to ponder on it, internalize it, and live its doctrines, principles, and precepts (D&C 84:54–57).

As a brief guided tour from First Nephi through Moroni, *When Ye Shall Receive These Things* is an invitation to meditate on the sweet and sobering word of the Lord found in the Book of Mormon, a summons to "try the virtue of the word of God" (Alma 31:5). We hope that through reflecting daily upon a single passage from the Book of Mormon, you will discover "new writing" (1 Nephi 16:29)—new truths, new insights, new perspectives—that will prove as stimulating to the mind as they are soothing and settling to the heart.

In the preparation of this volume, we are indebted to many people. Jana Erickson offered enthusiastic encouragement from the beginning. Lori Soza labored diligently to prepare the manuscript, and Suzanne Brady of Deseret Book Company provided her delicate, deliberate, and always sensitive editorial touch. We are grateful for our sweet wives, Karmel and Shauna, as well as our children, our own "stripling warriors," and for their love and support.

January

The fulness of mine intent is that I
may persuade men to come unto
the God of Abraham, and the
God of Isaac, and the God of
Jacob, and be saved.

1 Nephi 6:4

*I, Nephi, having been born of goodly parents, . . . and having seen
many afflictions in the course of my days, . . . yea, having had a
great knowledge of the goodness and the mysteries of God,
therefore I make a record of my proceedings in my days.*

1 NEPHI 1:1

Nephi was taught by loving and inspired parents;
that is, he was brought up "in the nurture and admo-
nition of the Lord" (Enos 1:1). Such teaching enabled
him to face life's afflictions with confidence and assurance, knowing in whom he trusted and knowing full
well that God would see him through any and all challenges. He was thus favored of the Lord to gain great
knowledge of the goodness and mysteries of God,
sacred truths that can be known only by the power of
the Holy Ghost. Each of us, if we are faithful, will
come to know firsthand of the goodness of God, will
experience his favor. And oh, what a blessing it is to
those who follow us—our posterity and other loved
ones—if we record in our journals the great lesson of
life, the lesson set forth in the Book of Mormon again
and again: God prospers those who keep his commandments. This is an eternal principle, a timeless
truth.

It came to pass in the commencement of the first year of the reign of Zedekiah, king of Judah, (my father, Lehi, having dwelt at Jerusalem in all his days); and in that same year there came many prophets, prophesying unto the people that they must repent, or the great city Jerusalem must be destroyed.

1 NEPHI 1:4

Lehi's call to serve as a prophet came in the first year in the reign of Zedekiah, approximately 600 B.C. God called Lehi just as he called several other prophets during that era—Jeremiah, Ezekiel, Daniel, and many others—to raise a voice of warning to a people steeped in idolatry and wickedness. We are not told, either in the Book of Mormon or in the Old Testament, just how these prophets were linked to one other, but understanding that God's house is a house of order, we conclude that each of them acted under divine direction from the Almighty and also under the directing power of one holding the keys, or right, of presidency.

*Overcome with the Spirit, he [Lehi] was carried away in a vision,
. . . and he thought he saw God sitting upon his throne,
surrounded with numberless concourses of angels in
the attitude of singing and praising their God.*

1 NEPHI 1:8

The apostle Paul wrote that no man takes unto himself the honor of priesthood ordination or divine call; no one, for example, calls himself to be a prophet (Hebrews 5:4). After Lehi received his prophetic commission, he was, like his colleagues Isaiah (Isaiah 6) and Ezekiel (Ezekiel 1), caught up into the presence of the Lord to behold the glory and majesty of God. He was then prepared to lead a new dispensation and convey to the world of his day the knowledge of God and the plan of salvation. Though we ourselves may not be caught up to the throne of God in this life, each of us is entitled to receive divine direction and empowerment from him whose work this is. We do not call ourselves to the work. God is our Principal; we are his agents and are on his errand. Whatever we do according to the will of the Lord is his business (D&C 64:29). Whom God calls, he qualifies.

When the Jews heard these things they . . . sought his life. . . . But behold, I, Nephi, will show unto you that the tender mercies of the Lord are over all those whom he hath chosen, because of their faith, to make them mighty even unto the power of deliverance.

1 NEPHI 1:20

Prophets and true disciples before and after Lehi and Nephi have been mocked, rejected, and slain by those who deny truth and embrace evil. But the merciful hand of the Lord is forever over his servants. He will make blessings of their afflictions for those who walk the path of righteousness (D&C 122:7). When we are on the Lord's errand, when we exercise steadfast faith in him, we will be strengthened in adversity and delivered from affliction. Nephi observed, "The commandments of God must be fulfilled. And if it so be that the children of men keep the commandments of God he doth nourish them, and strengthen them, and provide means whereby they can accomplish the thing which he has commanded them" (1 Nephi 17:3). The course of wickedness, however, offers no promises for protection, comfort, or peace: "The devil will not support his children at the last day, but doth speedily drag them down to hell" (Alma 30:60).

Laman and Lemuel, being the eldest, did murmur against their father. And they did murmur because they knew not the dealings of that God who had created them.

1 NEPHI 2:12

It is easy to complain when we do not see the full picture. Like Laman and Lemuel, too many of us murmur and find fault when we lack the details or are unable to perceive the quiet and often mysterious workings of the Lord and his servants. God does not call upon us to act in blind obedience, for dynamic discipleship demonstrates intelligent obedience. Rather than judge situations that may seem to be out of line to us, we would do well to humble ourselves, seek divine guidance and perspective, and perhaps even converse with those charged to direct us.

I, Nephi, . . . having great desires to know of the mysteries of God, wherefore, I did cry unto the Lord; and behold he did visit me, and did soften my heart that I did believe all the words which had been spoken by my father.

1 NEPHI 2:16

Nephi's desires to know of the mysteries of God were not unhealthy yearnings to know things that God purposely reserves to himself. Rather, Nephi desired simply to know things that can be known only by the power of the Spirit of God (1 Corinthians 2:11–14). God must be revealed, or he remains forever unknown. In the truest sense, then, we do not come to know the mysteries of God by exercising an excessive zeal, being caught up in gospel hobbies, or seeking to be truer than true. Like Nephi, we cry unto the Lord, pray to understand the things God would have us know, stay in the mainstream of the Church, and wait upon the Lord patiently. Eventually there will come to us quiet moments in which our hearts tell us things we did not know before. Further, God softens our hearts and thereby enables us to be open to additional promptings and direction.

*I, Nephi, said unto my father: I will go and do the things which
the Lord hath commanded, for I know that the Lord
giveth no commandments unto the children of men, save he shall
prepare a way for them that they may accomplish
the thing which he commandeth them.*

1 NEPHI 3:7

Nephi's faithful response to the Lord's command may be the most quoted verse in all scripture. Children and adults alike take courage from his unwavering answer: "I will go; I will do the thing the Lord commands" (*Children's Songbook,* 121). Nephi never vacillated, never wavered. Once assured of the Lord's will, he set forth to do it, moving forward one step at a time as directed by the peaceful nudging of the Spirit. And so must we. We may not fully comprehend the means, but the Lord will tell us (in our mind and in our heart) how to accomplish his ends (D&C 8:2). Quietly and deliberately we can proceed, trusting that we will receive more light and knowledge. With confidence in the Lord and his purposes, we can walk into an unknown future. When we want to obey, when we exercise faith, we have the promise of the Lord: He will provide a way.

*It is wisdom in God that we should obtain these records,
that we may preserve unto our children the language of our
fathers; and also that we may preserve unto them the words which
have been spoken by the mouth of all the holy prophets.*

1 NEPHI 3:19–20

The Lord knew that Lehi's family would need a scriptural record for their spiritual and intellectual preservation as a nation. Not only would their language be perpetuated, but the brass plates would be vital for recollecting the teachings of the prophets that had been handed down "since the world began" (1 Nephi 3:20). A spiritual legacy was contained in these sacred plates, and it needed to be given to its rightful heirs. Later in the Book of Mormon we learn the poignant history of the Mulekites, who failed to progress because of their spiritual and intellectual illiteracy, a condition due in part to the lack of a written record (Omni 1:17; Mosiah 1:3). We need the scriptures to be truly alive. All the prophets testify of sacred truths that are essential unto salvation. But their words sustain us only when we feast upon them, treasure them, and live them.

After the angel had departed, Laman and Lemuel again began to murmur, saying: How is it possible that the Lord will deliver Laban into our hands? Behold, he is a mighty man, and he can command fifty, yea, even he can slay fifty; then why not us?

1 NEPHI 3:31

One can have the heavens open, behold angels, have visions and dreams, even see the Lord himself, and yet not be converted. Because Laman and Lemuel had hardened their hearts against earlier spiritual promptings, there was no guarantee that a visit from a heavenly being would change their dispositions or direction. The Lord Jesus and his servants have repeatedly taught us of the need to put off the natural man and put on Christ, to become as a little child: submissive, meek, humble, patient, full of love, and willing to submit (Mosiah 3:19). Nephi and Sam laid their personal egos on the altar of God and found their hearts softened; Laman and Lemuel were unwilling to surrender themselves to the Lord and, tragically, remained in their lost and fallen state.

I was led by the Spirit, not knowing
beforehand the things which I should do.

1 NEPHI 4:6

The angel commanded Nephi and his brothers, "Behold ye shall go up to Jerusalem again, and the Lord will deliver Laban into your hands" (1 Nephi 3:29). Nephi trusted this instruction, nothing doubting. But it took more than positive thinking to accomplish such a divine directive. Bolstered by the Spirit of the Lord, he made his way along the darkened but familiar streets of Jerusalem, now more a foreigner than a citizen. The stakes were high. But he knew whose errand he was on. He listened for the still, small voice and humbly expected to be led. He had treasured up the words of eternal life, and now in this hour of need, he would be blessed for his faithfulness (D&C 84:85). Like Nephi, as we humbly yet courageously step to the edge of the light, seeking divine direction, and living so that we are qualified to receive it, we will be guided each step of the way.

The Spirit said unto me again: Slay him, for the Lord hath delivered him into thy hands; behold the Lord slayeth the wicked to bring forth his righteous purposes. It is better that one man should perish than that a nation should dwindle and perish in unbelief.

1 NEPHI 4:12–13

Almost always a revelation from God will be rational—it will make sense and be in harmony with the laws of the land and the order of God's kingdom on earth. Once in a great while, however, he who is the Author of good may command his anointed servants the prophets to violate the very principles they teach. The Prophet Joseph Smith declared: "That which is wrong under one circumstance, may be, and often is, right under another. God said, 'Thou shalt not kill'; at another time He said, 'Thou shalt utterly destroy.' This is the principle on which the government of heaven is conducted—by revelation adapted to the circumstances in which the children of the kingdom are placed. Whatever God requires is right, no matter what it is, although we may not see the reason thereof till long after the events transpire. If we seek first the kingdom of God, all good things will be added" (*Teachings*, 256).

*[Zoram], supposing that I spake of the brethren of the church,
and that I was truly that Laban whom I had slain,
wherefore he did follow me.*

1 NEPHI 4:26

Joseph Smith may have revealed to us as much about
the past as he did about the future (Mosiah 8:17). As a
result of the enlightenment given us through the Book
of Mormon and the revelations of the Restoration, we
know that Christ's gospel is eternal and that Christian
prophets have declared Christian doctrines and
administered Christian ordinances since the days of
Adam. Though its history has been punctuated by
periods of apostasy, the Church of Jesus Christ has
been on the earth through most of earth's own history
in various dispensations. Elder Bruce R. McConkie
observed: "There was not so much as the twinkling of
an eye during the whole so-called pre-Christian Era
when the Church of Jesus Christ was not upon the
earth, organized basically in the same way it now is.
Melchizedek belonged to the Church; Laban was a
member; so also was Lehi, long before he left
Jerusalem" (*Doctrines of the Restoration*, 292).

*I know that I am a visionary man; for if I had not
seen the things of God in a vision I should not
have known the goodness of God.*
1 NEPHI 5:4

Lehi had seen a vision. He knew it, and he knew that
God knew it. Lehi could not deny what he knew to be
true. He could not rationalize his vision away with
thoughts of *What will become of my family? What will people
think? How do I do this?* Instead, like Noah, he courageously responded to God's direction, uprooted his
family, and set sail for an unknown future in a chosen
land. Like Joseph Smith, he led with vision and forti-
tude as he established an old faith in a new place and
taught the goodness of God. Without vision we perish (Proverbs 29:18), both individually and as a people.
Thanks be to God for prophets who preach righteousness, for seers who truly see, for revelators who
reveal hidden truth.

*[Lehi] was a descendant of Joseph . . . who was sold into Egypt,
and who was preserved by the hand of the Lord, that he might
preserve his father, Jacob. . . . And they were also led out of
captivity . . . by that same God who had preserved them.*
1 NEPHI 5:14–15

In addition to preaching the saving doctrine of
Christ and the plan of salvation, prophets teach the
children of God who they are and Whose they are.
Through prophets we learn that we are the spirit
children of the Almighty, Elohim, our Heavenly
Father, and also that we are sons and daughters of a
noble lineage, the lineage of Abraham, Isaac, and
Jacob. Those who come into the gospel covenant who
may not have been natural heirs to the blessings of
such a lineage are adopted into the royal family and
given access to the same blessings. During times of
apostasy, one of the plain and precious truths often
lost is a sense of covenant consciousness. The declaration of lineage in our patriarchal blessings is as much
a statement about who and what we were in our first
estate as it is about who we are now and what we may
yet become.

*The fulness of mine intent is that I may persuade men to come
unto the God of Abraham, and the God of Isaac, and the
God of Jacob, and be saved.*

1 NEPHI 6:4

Some records are more conducive to bringing people
unto Christ than others. Historical accounts of archeology, genealogy, and wars are interesting and important, but they may not bring us to the one true God.
On the smaller plates, Nephi was commanded to
concentrate on spiritual matters, the dealings and revelations of God with the family of Lehi (2 Nephi
5:29–33). Nephi and his descendants who had editorial responsibility for the plates were solemnly selective in what they recorded, always considering the
purpose for which this set of plates was written and
preserved. The Book of Mormon contains the fulness
of the everlasting gospel and was written, plainly and
simply, to bring people to Jehovah, our Christ and
Lord. Nephi understood that his duty was to write the
things of God to teach us what we must do to gain
peace in this life and eternal salvation in the life to
come.

*Yea, and how is it that ye have forgotten that the Lord is able to
do all things according to his will, for the children of men,
if it so be that they exercise faith in him?
Wherefore, let us be faithful to him.*

1 NEPHI 7:12

How could Laman and Lemuel forget they had seen an angel? How could they forget how the Lord had delivered them out of the hands of Laban? How could they continue to harden their hearts and rebel against the Lord and their faithful younger brother in the face of so many witnesses to the power of God? Perhaps it is not so much in forgetting as in hardening. A hard heart is a forgetting heart. A hard heart is a rebellious heart. When the heart is hard, the things of the Spirit cannot enter the heart or mind. When the heart is hard, walls of forgetfulness emerge around all the spiritual impulses and memories, the things that turn our hearts to heaven. When we truly exercise faith in the Lord and sincerely believe him, we see him for what he is: the Savior, *our* Savior, from the harsh realities and hard-heartedness of the world.

*I did frankly forgive them all that they had done, and I did exhort
them that they would pray unto the Lord their God for
forgiveness. And it came to pass that they did so.*

1 NEPHI 7:21

Sorrow is a celestial feeling; forgiveness, a heavenly process. Nephi's soft heart quickly forgave as he desired the eternal welfare of his brothers. He could have felt justified in withholding his forgiveness; he could have lashed back in recrimination and punishment. Instead, he humbly forgave. But it was not the easy forgiveness of quick-fix remorse. He exhorted his brothers to sincerely pray, to repent, to plead for forgiveness from him through whom cleansing and lasting change comes. Nephi understood the Lord's command: "Forgive one another; for he that forgiveth not his brother his trespasses standeth condemned before the Lord; for there remaineth in him the greater sin. I, the Lord, will forgive whom I will forgive, but of you it is required to forgive all men" (D&C 64:9–10). Those with soft hearts can love and forgive even the hard-hearted.

*It came to pass that while my father tarried in the wilderness he
spake unto us, saying: Behold, I have dreamed a dream;
or, in other words, I have seen a vision.*
1 NEPHI 8:2

The Lord communicates with his children in a myriad of ways. Sometimes, as in the case of Joseph Smith, He reveals himself directly, in person. He speaks by and through the still small voice, infuses our intellect with pure intelligence, places feelings and impressions within our heart, sends angelic messengers, and even parts the heavens in an open vision. On occasions he makes known his mind and will through inspired dreams. Such individuals as Jacob, Joseph of old, Pharaoh, Nebuchadnezzar, Lehi, and Joseph the carpenter learned the will of heaven in this manner. Although not all dreams are visions, some visions do come through dreams. Whether man is awake or asleep, God uses every occasion he can to instruct and inspire.

*They did . . . commence in the path which led to the tree. And . . .
there arose a mist of darkness; yea, even an exceedingly great mist
of darkness, insomuch that they who had commenced in the path
did lose their way, that they wandered off and were lost.*

1 NEPHI 8:22–23

Lehi observed that many people had made their way onto the strait and narrow path, only to be met soon by mists of darkness, or "the temptations of the devil, which blindeth the eyes, and hardeneth the hearts of the children of men, and leadeth them away into broad roads, that they perish and are lost" (1 Nephi 12:17). Not being well enough grounded in truth, they wandered and were lost. The allures of wealth or fame or immorality can be so enticing that the steady beacon of the gospel can seem almost boring or unrewarding to the novice. That is, until disappointment and heartache set in. We all yearn for lasting peace, joy, love—all the fruit of the Spirit. But such heavenly rewards endure only as long as we do. We must forsake the world and grasp the iron rod firmly with both hands. With eyes fixed on the Lord, we can partake of his love and blessings—eternally.

I beheld others pressing forward, and they came forth and caught hold of the end of the rod of iron; and they did press forward through the mist of darkness, clinging to the rod of iron, even until they did come forth and partake of the fruit of the tree.

1 NEPHI 8:24

Although everyone wants to be loved and admired, in the eternal scheme of things it matters precious little what others think when it comes to our most significant decisions in life. There is a price to be paid for coming into the covenant gospel, and sometimes that price is the approval of those whose opinions matter to us. The single-minded disciple is able to take the fruit of the tree of life (partake of the powers of the Atonement) and move along the gospel path without distraction, caring little about what others think. In the language of Jacob, brother of Nephi, the Saints of the Holy One of Israel "have endured the crosses of the world, and despised the shame of it" (2 Nephi 9:18). That is to say, true conversion empowers one to ignore the tauntings and ridicule and scorn that emanate from those in the great and spacious buildings of this world.

He saw other multitudes pressing forward; and they came and
caught hold of the end of the rod of iron; and they did press their
way forward, continually holding fast to the rod of iron,
until they came forth and fell down
and partook of the fruit of the tree.

1 NEPHI 8:30

In his vision of the postmortal spirit world, President Joseph F. Smith beheld "an innumerable company of the spirits of the just, who had been faithful in the testimony of Jesus while they lived in mortality" (D&C 138:12). Although many of our Father's children will yield to the persuasions of worldly men and women, far more of the children of God will come to the truth, embrace the truth, devote their lives to the truth, and qualify for exaltation in the highest heaven than we might suppose. That is, God will be victorious. We have been instructed that through the cleansing powers of the blood of Christ, through the quiet but persistent pull of the everlasting covenant, and through the mercy and long-suffering of an omniloving God, multitudes, as Lehi saw, will inherit celestial glory. Truly, as the prophet Paul exulted, "Thanks be to God, which giveth us the victory through our Lord Jesus Christ" (1 Corinthians 15:57).

*He also saw other multitudes feeling their way towards that great
and spacious building. . . . many were drowned in the depths of
the fountain; and many were lost from his view, wandering in
strange roads. And great was the multitude that did
enter into that strange building.*

1 Nephi 8:31–33

The last group of people in Lehi's dream didn't even
try the path to the tree of life or the love of God. They
were "feeling their way" toward the strange building,
grasping blindly for anything that might satisfy their
selfish appetites. More than anything, they wanted to
get in on the action at the great and spacious building,
to rub shoulders with the worldly wise, the arrogant,
and affluent. But many did not get there; they were
consumed by their iniquity en route, lost along carnal
and sensual dead ends, sure that they knew a better
way. Such pride is at the root of all wickedness, even
self-righteousness. Just as we can be blinded by other
sins, we can become blinded by vanity. In contrast,
those who seek the path of discipleship, who humbly
submit their will to God's, are those who see things as
they really are. They look at the great and spacious
building and see it for all it is not.

The Lord knoweth all things from the beginning; wherefore, he prepareth a way to accomplish all his works among the children of men; for behold, he hath all power unto the fulfilling of all his words.

1 NEPHI 9:6

Nephi was commanded to keep both the large and the small plates for a wise purpose in the Lord. One purpose was realized in 1828, when Joseph Smith, through Martin Harris, lost the first 116 manuscript pages of the Book of Mormon, which had been translated from the large plates. At that point the Lord commanded Joseph Smith to translate material from the small plates covering about the same time period as that which had been lost (1 Nephi 6; Words of Mormon 1:5–7; D&C 10). Indeed, the Lord knows all things from the beginning. His plans cannot be thwarted by evil designs or inadvertent mistakes. In the same way, we can find wise purpose for our lives. As children of God, we are here to fulfill our unique mission. The Lord and his prophets charge us to live up to the divinity within us, to rely on his matchless power and tender mercy to become all that he intends for us to become.

Yea, even six hundred years from the time that my father left
Jerusalem, a prophet would the Lord God raise up
among the Jews—even a Messiah, or, in other words,
a Savior of the world.

1 NEPHI 10:4

The time of the Lord's first coming, like the precise time of his second coming in glory, was a set and fixed time. Prophets taught that in six hundred years (literally, in the meridian of time) Jesus would be born into mortality (1 Nephi 19:8; 2 Nephi 25:19). This prophesied coming of the Prophet of prophets, our Savior and Redeemer, would become the event by which time was measured thereafter. The word *Messiah* is from the Hebrew word meaning "anointed one." Jesus Christ was the One anointed, foreordained, and set apart to lift all mankind from the grave and to save all who would be saved. When he comes again, every knee will bow and every tongue confess that he is the anointed Prophet (Mosiah 27:31). In him and in the hope of his glory, we find rest for our souls.

Wherefore, all mankind were in a lost and in a fallen state, and ever would be save they should rely on this Redeemer.

1 NEPHI 10:6

The Latter-day Saint view of the Fall is remarkably optimistic. We believe that Adam and Eve went into the Garden to fall and that the Fall was as much a part of the foreordained plan of the Father as the Atonement. Elder Orson F. Whitney taught, "The Fall had a twofold direction—downward, yet forward. It brought man into the world and set his feet upon progression's highway" (*Cowley and Whitney on Doctrine,* 287). Further, the scriptures of the Restoration affirm that Adam and Eve were forgiven of their transgression in the Garden of Eden and thus "the Son of God hath atoned for original guilt" (Moses 6:54). At the same time, however, there was a fall, and this fall does indeed take its toll upon us, both physically and spiritually. As Lehi observed, all men and women remain in a lost and fallen state unless and until they rely upon the redeeming powers of Jesus Christ (1 Nephi 10:6).

*After the Gentiles had received the fulness of the Gospel,
the natural branches of the olive-tree, or the remnants of the
house of Israel, should be grafted in, or come to the knowledge of
the true Messiah, their Lord and their Redeemer.*

1 NEPHI 10:14

All things bear witness of Christ (Moses 6:63). The scattering and gathering of the house of Israel is a type and a shadow of the fall of man and the atonement of Jesus Christ. Just as individuals fall through disobedience, so Israel (as individuals, as well as a nation) are scattered when they reject the true Messiah and his gospel. On the other hand, just as individuals enjoy the cleansing powers of the Atonement and association with the household of faith when they repent and are forgiven, so the house of Israel are gathered to Christ and to the lands of their inheritance (the congregations of the faithful) when they come unto Christ and receive his everlasting covenant. Like natural branches, the penitent are grafted into the tree of Christ when they come to know the true Messiah.

He that diligently seeketh shall find; and the mysteries of God shall be unfolded unto them, by the power of the Holy Ghost, as well in these times as in times of old, and as well in times of old as in times to come; wherefore, the course of the Lord is one eternal round.

1 NEPHI 10:19

The apostle Peter taught that "God is no respecter of persons: but in every nation he that feareth him, and worketh righteousness, is accepted with him" (Acts 10:34–35). The Prophet Joseph Smith explained that "even the least Saint may know all things as fast as he is able to bear them" (*Teachings,* 149). God is everlastingly the same—he is constant, consistent, generous, and eager to share light and truth and knowledge with those who seek him earnestly. Those who receive the gift of the Holy Ghost and cultivate the Spirit within their lives are entitled to have the things of God unfolded unto them, according to their own needs and circumstances as well as the mind and will of God (D&C 88:68). The Savior eloquently stated this principle: "I, the Lord, am merciful and gracious unto those who fear me, and delight to honor those who serve me in righteousness and truth unto the end" (D&C 76:5).

*After I had desired to know the things that my father had seen,
and believing that the Lord was able to make them known unto
me, as I sat pondering in mine heart I was caught away in the
Spirit of the Lord, yea, into an exceedingly high mountain.*

1 NEPHI 11:1

Meditative pondering is a form of sacred devotion, a
quiet and effective means by which we can draw near to
the Infinite and become partakers of spiritual gifts. True
disciples know this power. Nephi linked pondering with
scripture reading: "My soul delighteth in the scriptures,
and my heart pondereth them. . . . Behold, my soul
delighteth in the things of the Lord; and my heart pondereth continually upon the things which I have seen and
heard" (2 Nephi 4:15–16). Through his pondering and
sincere desiring, Nephi was transported to another
place—a high mountain, often thought of as nature's
temple—wherein he could experience the manifold
things God desired him to experience. Moses received a
similar kind of instruction (Moses 1:1), as did Philip (Acts
8:39) and Jesus himself (JST Matthew 4:1–11). Pondering
unlocks the door to revelation. Deep reflection upon the
things of God can open the windows of heaven (D&C
76:19; 138:1–3, 11; Joseph Smith–History 1:11–12).

The Spirit said unto me: Believest thou that thy father saw the tree of which he hath spoken? And I said: Yea. . . . the Spirit cried with a loud voice, saying: . . . blessed art thou, Nephi, because thou believest in the Son of the most high God.

1 NEPHI 11:4–6

While pondering upon the things which his father had taught, Nephi was caught away in the Spirit of the Lord to an exceedingly high mountain. There he received a panoramic vision, an overview of the workings of the Almighty to the end of time (1 Nephi 11–14). Nephi declared to the Spirit his own desires to see the things which his father had seen and his belief in all that his father had taught him, including the significance of the tree of life. But faith is not exercised in trees, and the Spirit was not simply inquiring into Nephi's knowledge of a form of plant life. The tree is obviously a doctrinal symbol, a sign of an even greater reality. It has been a symbol, even from the time of the Edenic paradise, of the central and saving role of Jesus Christ.

He said unto me: Knowest thou the condescension of God?
And I said unto him: I know that he loveth his children;
nevertheless, I do not know the meaning of all things.
1 NEPHI 11:16–17

Nephi was here asked the question of the ages, not unlike the query posed some six hundred years later by the Master himself: "What think ye of Christ?" (Matthew 22:42). Nephi was a righteous man, a son of God who had learned many things concerning the condescension of God. In his humility, however, he delivered a sweet concession that he did not know all things and offered to us a principle that will see us through the perils and poignant difficulties of life: the simple but profound truth that God loves his children. We need not have all the answers. We need not understand the reasons for this tragedy or that trauma. Until the Lord sees fit to reveal all things, it is sufficient to know that God is indeed our Father in Heaven, that he is aware of us, that he orchestrates the events of our lives, and that his love and tender regard for us is perfect and infinite.

I know that he [God] loveth his children.
1 NEPHI 11:17

So much about life can be uncertain. Sometimes we have to hold in abeyance those things that are beyond our capacity to understand. Death, disease, heartbreak, and loneliness can fill our days and keep us awake at night. From our limited perspective, present pain can feel overwhelming at times. But rising above despair and grief, ascending over the confusion and uncertainties of life, is the immutable assurance: God neither slumbers nor sleeps as he watches over his children (Psalm 121:4). The majesty of it all is unfathomable to our finite minds. The infinite and marvelous love made manifest by the Father and the Son is incomprehensible. But just as we do not need to fully understand gravity or electricity to know that they are real and powerful, so we do not have to know *all* things to know this *one* thing: Our Heavenly Father loves each one of us, his sons and daughters.

FEBRUARY

*He that diligently seeketh shall
find; and the mysteries of God
shall be unfolded unto them, by the
power of the Holy Ghost.*

1 NEPHI 10:19

The angel said unto me: Behold the Lamb of God, yea, even the
Son of the Eternal Father! Knowest thou the meaning
of the tree which thy father saw?
1 NEPHI 11:21

It was as if the angel were summing up, bringing Nephi back to the point where he had begun—pondering the deeper significance of the tree. Having shown Nephi the virgin bearing the child in her arms, the angel asked him, in essence, "Now do you understand the meaning of the tree?" Nephi answered from understanding given by the power of the Spirit. The tree represented more than an abstract emotion, more than a sentiment (albeit a divine one). The tree represented the greatest manifestation of charity, the pure love of Christ—in truth, the very gift of Christ. "For God so loved the world, that he gave his only begotten Son, that whosoever believeth in him should not perish, but have everlasting life" (John 3:16).

It came to pass that I beheld that the rod of iron, which my father had seen, was the word of God, which led to the fountain of living waters, or to the tree of life; which waters are a representation of the love of God.

1 Nephi 11:25

Nephi explained to his brothers that "whoso would hearken unto the word of God, and would hold fast to it, they would never perish; neither could the temptations and the fiery darts of the adversary overpower them unto blindness, to lead them away to destruction" (1 Nephi 15:24). From the beginning, the Lord has established the way whereby we can find safety from the winds of adversity and the allures of this world. As we learn and live the gospel, we feel God's love. Holding fast to the rod of iron, which is the gospel of Jesus Christ, we progress to the end of the strait and narrow path. There we find the tree of life and the fountain of living water, both symbols of Jesus Christ, who is himself the greatest manifestation of God's love for us. In him our thirst can be forever quenched (Jeremiah 2:13), for he is the "well of water springing up into everlasting life" (John 4:14).

I beheld the Lamb of God going forth among the children of men.
And I beheld multitudes of people who were sick, and who were
afflicted with all manner of diseases, and with devils and unclean
spirits. . . . And they were healed by the power of the Lamb of God.

I NEPHI 11:31

Like Nephi of old, President Gordon B. Hinckley has borne testimony of Jesus Christ. President Hinckley declared: "I know that I am not the head of this Church. The Lord Jesus Christ is its head. He is its living head. My mission, my chief responsibility, my greatest honor comes in bearing solemn testimony of His living reality. Jesus Christ is the Son of God, who condescended to come into this world of misery, struggle, and pain, to touch men's hearts for good, to teach the way of eternal life, and to give Himself as a sacrifice for the sins of all mankind. . . . How different, how empty our lives would be without Him. How much truer, how much deeper is our love and appreciation and respect one for another because of Him. . . . I bear solemn witness that He lives and stands on the right hand of His Father" (*Teachings of Gordon B. Hinckley*, 285–86).

The great and spacious building was the pride of the world; and it
fell, and the fall thereof was exceedingly great. And the angel
of the Lord spake unto me again, saying: Thus shall be the
destruction of all nations, kindreds, tongues, and people,
that shall fight against the twelve apostles of the Lamb.

1 NEPHI 11:36

It is not alone the Gentiles who put to death the
Lord of life, nor people from outside the chosen lineage who persecute the Saints of the Most High.
Tragically, it is the people of the covenant, those called
in premortality who do not now merit chosen status,
who murder the Mediator of the new covenant and
malign the members of his society. The latter-day
kingdom is little hindered by those from outside it
who are bent upon its destruction. External persecution seems to strengthen the flock and even to pro-
voke the interest of the investigator. More damage is
done by those who have professed to know the name
of the Lord and yet have not known him, those who
blaspheme against God in the midst of his house
(D&C 112:26). In the long run, "there is no weapon
that is formed against you shall prosper; and if any
man lift his voice against you he shall be confounded"
(D&C 71:9–10).

The angel said unto me: Look! And I looked, and beheld three
generations pass away in righteousness; and their garments were
white even like unto the Lamb of God. And the angel said unto
me: These are made white in the blood of the Lamb,
because of their faith in him.

1 NEPHI 12:11

The word *baptism* implies immersion and entails the
creation of a new identity. To be baptized unto Christ
is not only to be immersed in water but also to gain a
new identification with the Savior and the sheep of his
fold. There is a terrible irony associated with becoming clean through having our garments washed white
in the blood of the Lamb. The dross and iniquity of
the human soul is remitted and removed through the
atoning blood of Christ, the Lord Omnipotent: "For
the life of the flesh is in the blood: and I have given it
to you upon the altar to make an atonement for your
souls; for it is the blood that maketh an atonement for
the soul" (Leviticus 17:11).

I saw among the nations of the Gentiles the formation of a great
church . . . which is most abominable above all churches, which
slayeth the saints of God, yea, . . . and bringeth them down into
captivity. . . . And I saw the devil that he was the founder of it.

1 NEPHI 13:4–6

The great and abominable church, the whore of all
the earth, consists of individuals and organizations
who knowingly choose to fight against Zion and seek
to thwart the spread of the kingdom of God (2 Nephi
10:16). As a part of his panoramic vision, Nephi sees
what might be called the historic great and abominable church, what we have come to know as hell-
enized Christianity, the Christian church that fell into
apostasy in the centuries after the crucifixion of Christ
and the deaths of the apostles. From Nephi's vantage
point, it is a great and spacious building that is lifted
high in the air—the devil is its foundation and there
is no truth in him (John 8:44).

I looked and beheld a man among the Gentiles . . . and I beheld
the Spirit of God, that it came down and wrought upon the man;
and he went forth upon the many waters, even unto the seed of
my brethren, who were in the promised land.

1 NEPHI 13:12

More than two thousand years before Columbus set
sail, Nephi saw in vision the discovery and colonizing of
the Americas, events that were vital to the Restoration.
Columbus acknowledged that the Holy Ghost inspired
him on his journey and the Lord gave him courage and
understanding. President Ezra Taft Benson declared:
"The destiny of America was divinely decreed. The
events which established our great nation were foreknown to God and revealed to prophets of old. As in an
enacted drama, the players who came on the scene were
rehearsed and selected for their parts. Their talents, abilities, capacities, and weaknesses were known before they
were born. As one looks back upon what we call our
history, there is a telling theme which recurs again and
again in this drama. It is that God governs in the affairs
of this nation" ("God's Hand in Our Nation's History,"
298). All things, both globally and individually, are
known to him who is omniscient and eternal.

Their mother Gentiles were gathered together . . . to battle against them. And I beheld that the power of God was with them, and . . . the Gentiles that had gone out of captivity were delivered by the power of God out of the hands of all other nations.

1 Nephi 13: 17–19

The Book of Mormon makes clear that God helped the colonists to establish themselves in America by delivering them out of the hands of their "mother Gentiles." The land we call America plays an important role in God's plan for his children. This land was home to the place known as Eden (Bible Dictionary, s.v. "Eden") and will one day be the New Jerusalem (Article of Faith 10). This land has been set apart for wise and special purposes: this is the place where the dispensation of the fulness of times could be ushered in, the place where the ancient record would be found, the place that prophets have had their eyes on for millennia. When we consider why and how this land has been preserved, we feel the sobering realization that much is expected of those who abide in it. We must do our part to strengthen and uphold this foreordained land.

*Thou seest that after the book hath gone forth through the hands
of the great and abominable church, that there are many plain
and precious things taken away from the book, which is
the book of the Lamb of God.*

1 NEPHI 13:28

Far more important than exactly who or what consti-
tutes the great and abominable church is what that
nefarious organization does: it persecutes, tortures, and
enslaves the Saints, and it systematically takes away
many plain and precious truths from the scriptures,
meaning the Bible. These actions create stumbling
blocks for those who seek to understand the stick of
Judah, for transcendent truths have been removed: the
personal and corporeal nature of God the Father; the
infinite scope and breadth of Christ's atoning sacrifice;
the delicate balance between the grace of God and the
works of man; the nature of Christ's eternal gospel; the
necessity of priesthood authority, covenants, and ordinances; the central saving place of holy temples; the premortal and postmortal existence of man; degrees of
glory in the hereafter; and the eternal family unit. We
are able to gauge the importance of what has been
removed from scripture by attending carefully to what
God in his mercy and wisdom has chosen to restore.

*These last records . . . shall establish the truth of the first, which
are of the twelve apostles of the Lamb, . . . and shall make known
to all . . . that the Lamb of God is the Son of the Eternal
Father, . . . and that all men must come unto him,
or they cannot be saved.*

1 NEPHI 13:40

Though we are sobered by the realization that
sacred doctrinal truths are not available to the world
at large, we rejoice with Nephi in the times of restitu-
tion, the days of restoration, in which plain and precious truths are returned to earth through modern
scripture and living apostles and prophets. The Book
of Mormon itself is clearly one of the means by which
lost doctrine is restored. The God of heaven chooses
also to bring forth other scriptures, which certainly
includes the Doctrine and Covenants, the Pearl of
Great Price, Joseph Smith's Translation of the Bible,
and additional truth from living prophets. These other
sacred records affirm the historical veracity and essential truthfulness of the Bible and testify, in tandem
with the Book of Mormon, that Jesus Christ is the
Son of God and the Savior of all humankind.

*Behold there are save two churches only; the one is the church of
the Lamb of God, and the other is the church of the devil.*

1 NEPHI 14:10

Nephi saw the great and abominable church in the
period following the New Testament era and also in
the latter days. With the establishment of the Church
in this dispensation, an organization was again on earth
with the authority to preach the gospel and administer
the ordinances thereof. By divine testimony, it is the
"only true and living church upon the face of the whole
earth" (D&C 1:30). Certainly, light, truth, and goodness can be found outside the Church, but eternal life is
found nowhere else. Salvation is not a congregational
process, anyway; for those within the Church or outside it, salvation is an individual course. In stating that
there are two churches only, the Lord speaks of the
opposing forces of good and evil, virtue and vice.
Lucifer would like to blur the line between good and
evil and lead us along a wrong path. We must do all in
our power to remain faithful to the truth and help to
bring the Lord's sheep into his fold.

*I beheld the church of the Lamb of God, and its numbers were
few, because of the wickedness and abominations of the
whore who sat upon many waters.*
1 NEPHI 14:12

At any given time it may appear as though Satan is
winning the war for the souls of men and women. His
followers are legion, and his diabolical tactics become
more and more sophisticated and rampant as time
passes. Yet, the church of the Lamb of God will continue to grow, missionaries by the hundreds of thousands will spread the message of truth to every corner
of the earth, and millions will respond to the quiet
promptings of the Spirit to come into the faith
through conversion. At the same time, the number of
persons within the church of the Lamb on earth will
be relatively few when compared to the numbers
within the church of the devil. But eventually the victory will be the Lord's, and righteousness will prevail
when the Lord of Hosts in his might returns to begin
his millennial reign.

I, Nephi, beheld the power of the Lamb of God, that it descended upon the saints of the church of the Lamb, . . . who were scattered upon all the face of the earth; and they were armed with righteousness and with the power of God in great glory.

1 NEPHI 14:14

Too often we may be inclined to think that might makes right and that modern technology will ensure that right prevails on earth. Nephi's vision tells a different story. Here we learn that it will not be by the power of bombs and artillery and military strategy alone that the eventual victory over evil will be won but rather by and through the power of the Almighty that descends upon the Saints of the church of the Lamb and upon the covenant people of the Lord. The faithful, armed with righteousness, look to the Lord of hosts, the Lord of armies, for deliverance. John the Revelator saw the day in which the Lamb would overcome the enemies of righteousness, "for he is Lord of lords, and King of kings: and they that are with him are called, and chosen, and faithful" (Revelation 17:14).

I, Nephi, am forbidden that I should write the remainder
of the things which I saw and heard; wherefore the things
which I have written sufficeth me; and I have written
but a small part of the things which I saw.

1 NEPHI 14:28

The law of witnesses having been fulfilled, Nephi bears strong testimony that what he has written is true. His desire was righteous, his effort sincere, and he was blessed to know what his father knew. By divine decree he was restrained from sharing more, but he was content with the things the Lord allotted unto him (Alma 29:3). What a compelling vision was this "small part"! An angel of the Lord opened the doors of heaven, and light and truth distilled upon him like the dews of heaven (D&C 121:45). Ever obedient and faithful, Nephi retained heaven's trust by recording only that which he was permitted to share. For a wise purpose, he simply bore his witness and ended the record of his vision. Likewise, as we desire righteousness and revelation and faithfully do our part to be worthy of divine endowments, the still small voice of the Spirit whispers peace and understanding to our souls. We, too, can humbly bear record of truth.

I said unto them: Have ye inquired of the Lord?
And they said unto me: We have not; for the Lord
maketh no such thing known unto us.

1 NEPHI 15:8–9

Whether a murmuring spirit, laziness, or hard-heartedness, any spiritual malady can close the windows of heaven and rob us of the confidence we need to approach the Lord in faith that he will respond. Nephi exhorted his brothers by quoting the promise of the Lord, "If ye will not harden your hearts, and ask me in faith, believing that ye shall receive, with diligence in keeping my commandments, surely these things shall be made known unto you" (1 Nephi 15:11). The formula for personal revelation, while simple, is not easy. Predicated upon our having contrite hearts and obeying the commandments of God, personal revelation is the birthright of all who receive the Holy Ghost (Smith, *Teachings,* 328). The Lord invites us to ask in faith, nothing wavering (James 1:6). He commands us to have hearts that are broken in repentance (3 Nephi 9:20). He stands ready to respond to our sincere inquiries. But he cannot answer if we do not ask.

At that day shall the remnant of our seed know that they are of
the house of Israel, and that they are the
covenant people of the Lord.

1 NEPHI 15:14

One's covenant status entails more than lineal descent. Indeed, as the apostle Paul taught, "They are not all Israel, which are of Israel" (Romans 9:6; compare 2 Nephi 30:2). True Israelites are those who come to the Mediator of the covenant, learn his gospel, accept his doctrine, join his church, and congregate with the faithful. The gathering is first spiritual and then temporal. Both individually and as a nation, we are gathered first and foremost to a Person, not to a place.

I did rehearse unto them the words of Isaiah, who spake concerning the restoration of the Jews, or of the house of Israel; and after they were restored they should no more be confounded, neither should they be scattered again.

1 NEPHI 15: 20

Few prophecies concerning the destiny of the house of Israel relate solely to one group of people. Almost always the prophecies of Isaiah or Jeremiah or Ezekiel or Lehi or Nephi or Jacob or the risen Christ concerning the gathering of Israel pertain to all of Israel. Thus, in seeking to understand and interpret the prophetic word, we approach the scriptures with a broad perspective, knowing that God will, in his mysterious way, eventually bring about the conversion and settlement of all branches of his chosen people. Truly, "all are alike unto God" (2 Nephi 26:33).

Wherefore, the wicked are rejected from the righteous, and also from that tree of life, whose fruit is most precious and most desirable above all other fruits; yea, and it is the greatest of all the gifts of God.

1 NEPHI 15:36

Good cannot reconcile with evil, or it will cease to be good. In the same way, the fruit of the tree of life will be delicious only to those who refine their tastes in righteousness. Those who feast on the scriptures, partake of the Lord's emblems, and otherwise enjoy the fruits of the gospel come to "hunger and thirst after righteousness" (Matthew 5:6). God's greatest gifts are reserved for such. "If thou wilt do good," the Lord said to those of our dispensation, "yea, and hold out faithful to the end, thou shalt be saved in the kingdom of God, which is the greatest of all the gifts of God; for there is no gift greater than the gift of salvation" (D&C 6:13). This exalted life is reserved for those who are faithful and true to the plan of happiness, who believe Christ and follow him, who do all things "with an eye single to the glory of God" (D&C 82:19; 88:67).

I said unto them that I knew that I had spoken hard things
against the wicked, according to the truth; . . . wherefore,
the guilty taketh the truth to be hard, for it cutteth
them to the very center.

1 NEPHI 16:2

Hundreds of years after Nephi, the prophet
Abinadi, who was also protected by divine powers,
said, "Ye have not power to slay me, therefore I finish
my message. Yea, and I perceive that it cuts you to
your hearts because I tell you the truth concerning
your iniquities" (Mosiah 13:7). In our own day the
Lord has said, "Behold, I am God; give heed to my
word, which is quick and powerful, sharper than a
two-edged sword, to the dividing asunder of both
joints and marrow; therefore give heed unto my word"
(D&C 11:2). The righteous rejoice in the word of
God, whereas the wicked are offended by it. Light and
darkness will never be compatible; if we are in darkness, the bright light of truth may be difficult to
tolerate, unless we repent and forsake our sins. The
hard-hearted are offended by truth, but the softhearted find truth delicious to the soul. They willingly
make sacrifices to embrace the gospel and live it.

*I, Nephi, did make out of wood a bow, and out of a straight stick,
an arrow. . . . And I said unto my father: Whither shall I go to
obtain food? And it came to pass that he did inquire of the Lord,
for they had humbled themselves because of my words.*

1 NEPHI 16:23–24

Having traveled for many days, the little band of
sojourners needed food and rest. Nephi's steel bow
broke and his brothers' bows lost their spring. The
murmuring started anew. Even faithful Lehi, hungry
and fatigued, complained against the Lord. But Nephi
courageously took action. He made a bow and arrow
and, with deep sensitivity to the order of things and
to Lehi's heart, asked his father to seek inspiration in
finding game. Penitent and humbled, the family patriarch sought for guidance. The hearts of Nephi and of
Lehi are revealed here: fearless, Nephi goes forward
with faith but doesn't overstep his beloved father. By
so doing, he lovingly instructs. Lehi understands full
well that inspiration is not forthcoming to complainers and doubters. He meekly repents and receives the
asked-for guidance. What love he must have felt for
this son, whose faith bolstered his own during a weak
moment. Likewise, the Lord is pleased when we are
faithful, strong, and humble in the midst of adversity.

I, Nephi, beheld the pointers which were in the ball, that they did
work according to the faith and diligence and heed which we
did give unto them. . . . And thus we see that by small
means the Lord can bring about great things.

1 NEPHI 16:28–29

Guidance from the Spirit comes to us according to our faith in the Lord and our diligence in keeping his commandments. The Lord's messages are given at specific times for particular purposes, sometimes in "curious" ways (1 Nephi 16:10)—if we humbly seek divine direction and are prepared to receive it. President Gordon B. Hinckley stated: "There is no greater blessing that can come into our lives than the gift of the Holy Ghost—the companionship of the Holy Spirit to guide us, protect us, and bless us, to go, as it were, as a pillar before us and a flame to lead us in paths of righteousness and truth. That guiding power of the third member of the Godhead can be ours if we live worthy of it" (*Teachings of Gordon B. Hinckley*, 259). By small means the Lord can accomplish his great purposes in our lives.

*When they saw that I began to be sorrowful they were glad in
their hearts, insomuch that they did rejoice over me, saying:
We knew that ye could not construct a ship, for we knew
that ye were lacking in judgment; wherefore, thou
canst not accomplish so great a work.*

1 NEPHI 17:19

Naysayers, critics, and complainers have been with
us since the beginning of time. Nephi's announcement
that he and his brothers were to build a ship and then
cross the ocean was met with ridicule and contempt
from Laman and Lemuel. Even more distressing,
Laman and Lemuel rejoiced when they saw Nephi
sorrowing. But Nephi's sorrow came not from the
weight of the task ahead nor from the burden of
leadership—he had been commanded to build a ship,
and build a ship he would! His sorrow came from the
faithlessness of his brothers, the family pain they
caused with their continual murmuring. President
David O. McKay said, "In the Church we sometimes
find two groups of people: the builders and murmur-
ers. Let each ask himself: 'In which class should I be
placed?'" (*Improvement Era*, March 1969, 3). We are to go
forward with faith as we wholeheartedly follow the
Lord's leaders.

*Behold, the Lord esteemeth all flesh in one; he that is righteous is
favored of God. But behold, this people had rejected every word of
God, and they were ripe in iniquity; . . . and the Lord did curse
the land against them, and bless it unto our fathers.*

1 NEPHI 17:35

Our Heavenly Father loves all of his children. He
desires to bless and prosper each of us, but he is able
to do so only to the extent that we live the laws upon
which the blessings are predicated (D&C 130:20–21).
The full enjoyment of our Father's blessings depends
upon our faithfulness. Thus, as Nephi taught, though
the Lord does esteem all flesh in one, those who keep
the commandments are favored—smiled upon,
blessed, prospered (1 Nephi 17:35). To dramatize the
importance of staying on the Lord's side of the line,
the prophets often use startling language. Samuel the
Lamanite taught that God loved the "people of
Nephi" but "the Lamanites hath he hated because
their deeds have been evil continually" (Helaman
15:3–4). We must not misunderstand the intent of
such passages; God's love for his children is constant,
but his ability to lead, empower, and bring the deepest fulfillment into their lives comes only as they yield
their hearts to him.

*[The Lord] sent fiery flying serpents among them; and after they were
bitten he prepared a way that they might be healed; and the labor
which they had to perform was to look; and because of the simpleness
of the way, or the easiness of it, there were many who perished.*

1 NEPHI 17:41

Nephi reminded his brothers of what happened to
their forefathers when they spoke against God while
wandering in the wilderness. The Lord responded
with fiery serpents that had deadly venom. Fearing for
their lives, the Israelites pleaded with Moses: "We have
sinned, for we have spoken against the Lord, and
against thee; pray unto the Lord, that he take away the
serpents from us" (Numbers 21:7). In response to his
prayer, Moses was told to fashion a pole with the figure of a serpent on it. This was set before the people
with the promise that those who had been bitten by
the snakes could, by looking upon the pole, be healed
(Numbers 21:6–9). Nephi reminded his brothers that
many died, refusing to look upon the pole because it
seemed too simple a solution. This incident is a type
of the healing and salvation to be found in Christ. Let
us look to God and live (Alma 37:46–47).

Ye are swift to do iniquity but slow to remember the Lord your God. . . . ye have heard his voice from time to time; and he hath spoken unto you in a still small voice, but ye were past feeling, that ye could not feel his words.

1 NEPHI 17:45

The Lord described the spirit of revelation, "I will tell you in your mind and in your heart, by the Holy Ghost, which shall come upon you and which shall dwell in your heart" (D&C 8:2). That still small voice of truth and revelation cannot penetrate a hard and rebellious heart. Christ spoke of the inability of the wicked to "understand with their heart" (Matthew 13:15), whereas the righteous "understand in their hearts" things too marvelous to utter (3 Nephi 19:33). The spirit of truth is felt. It speaks softly, reassuringly; it feels good, uplifting, ennobling; it moves us to reach out to others in love and service; it inspires us to keep the Lord's commandments and seek to do his will in our lives. But to the wicked and callous of heart, the things of eternity are strange, forgotten, and ultimately rejected. The Lord wants us to be softhearted, contrite, and open to his gospel of salvation, his great plan of happiness.

*They said . . . we know that it is the power of the Lord that has
shaken us. And they fell down before me, and were about
to worship me, but I would not suffer them, saying: . . .
worship the Lord thy God.*
1 NEPHI 17:55

It is appropriate that we love and respect those whom the Lord has chosen as our leaders. We honor the offices they hold and fully sustain our leaders in their efforts. But it is wholly inappropriate for us to worship them or put them up on a pedestal of perfection. When Cornelius fell at the feet of Peter to worship him, Peter forbade him, saying, "Stand up; I myself also am a man" (Acts 10:26). When the people of Lystra attempted to worship Paul and Barnabas as gods, the apostles "rent their clothes" and cried out, saying, "Why do ye these things? We also are men of like passions with you, and preach unto you that ye should turn from these vanities unto the living God" (Acts 14:14–15). We worship Him who is perfect, the Lord our God.

I, Nephi, did go into the mount oft, and I did pray oft unto the Lord; wherefore the Lord showed unto me great things.

1 NEPHI 18:3

Nephi was a man of prayer. He instructed those of our day to "pray always" and "not [to] perform any thing unto the Lord save in the first place ye shall pray unto the Father in the name of Christ" (2 Nephi 32:9). Nephi had established a special place of prayer and revelation, a mount where he would often go to seek for divine help. The Lord showed him more than how to build a ship or how the group should make their journey. The Lord instructed him in the things of the Spirit (2 Nephi 4:25). Great things were shown Nephi because of his faithfulness—and because he prayed often. The Lord taught Nephi's contemporary Jeremiah, "Call unto me, and I will answer thee, and shew thee great and mighty things, which thou knowest not" (Jeremiah 33:3). The Lord cannot answer us if we don't ask; he will not show us great things if we are not faithful. We must live in righteousness and ask in faith.

*Nevertheless, I did look unto my God, and I did praise him all the
day long; and I did not murmur against the Lord
because of mine afflictions.*

1 NEPHI 18:16

To be hated and abused by loved ones causes the
deepest kind of pain. But Nephi remained steadfast and
immovable, praising the Lord and murmuring not, even
while bound in strong cords for four days. His brothers
ignored the fervent pleas of their family for mercy in his
behalf, the Liahona stopped working, and a terrible
storm came upon the water. But it wasn't until hard-
hearted Laman and Lemuel feared for their own lives
that they released their younger brother. As is often the
case, only selfishness caused them to desist. Through it
all, Nephi looked to God for strength, refrained from
complaint, and even praised God. Nephi's life teaches
us that things are rarely easy for the righteous. The Lord
desires that we develop the attributes of godliness, and
to do so, he refines and enlarges our souls—often
through trials and tribulations. These crucible experiences give us opportunities to test our mettle even while
we are being changed from the inside out.

*It came to pass that after we had sailed for the space of many days
we did arrive at the promised land; and we went forth
upon the land, and did pitch our tents; and we did
call it the promised land.*

1 NEPHI 18:23

I n 1 Nephi and in several other places in the Book of Mormon, the land of America is designated as a promised land. It is a land of promise in that it offers great promises to those who serve the God of this land, who is Jesus Christ (Ether 2:12). It is a promised land in that it was the place where life began on this planet, and it will be the place where the center stake of the New Jerusalem will be established before the second coming of the Son of Man. But a land of promise can remain a land of promise only to the extent that the people who inhabit it remain a people of promise, a covenant-keeping people, who hearken to the voice of the Lord (Abraham 2:6).

MARCH

*The gate by which ye should enter
is repentance and baptism by
water; and then cometh a
remission of your sins by fire and
by the Holy Ghost.*

2 NEPHI 31:17

The things which some men esteem to be of great worth, both to the body and soul, others set at naught and trample under their feet. Yea, even the very God of Israel do men trample under their feet . . . and hearken not to the voice of his counsels.

1 NEPHI 19:7

Sacred things are not esteemed by everyone. Those who have chosen to walk the gospel path and to cultivate the spirit of inspiration esteem the things of God to be of great worth, whereas the people of the world consider such matters foolish and irrelevant. The first look upon life with an eye of faith; the second view things through the myopic lenses of the natural man. The apostle Paul wrote, "I count all things but loss for the excellency of the knowledge of Christ Jesus my Lord: for whom I have suffered the loss of all things, and do count them but dung, that I may win Christ" (Philippians 3:8). Truly, "when we put God first, all other things fall into their proper place or drop out of our lives" (Ezra Taft Benson, *Ensign,* May 1988, 4). In the long run it matters precious little what others think. What really matters is what the Lord thinks: A proper perspective leads to proper priorities.

The God of our fathers . . . yieldeth himself . . . into the hands of
wicked men, to be lifted up, according to the words of Zenock, and
to be crucified, according to the words of Neum, and to be
buried in a sepulchre, according to the words of Zenos.

1 NEPHI 19:10

The brass plates were much more comprehensive than our present Old Testament (1 Nephi 13:23). The prophets whose words were recorded on the brass plates spoke clearly of the nature of God and the Godhead, the eternal gospel, and particulars concerning the death and resurrection of the Messiah. Today we must read the Old Testament through the lenses of the New Testament and modern revelation even to recognize the messianic allusions contained therein, but the Book of Mormon, which contains many of the teachings in the brass plates, is clearly gospel-centered and Christ-centered. Zenos, Zenock, Neum, and Ezias (Helaman 8:20) knew of and preached of the Savior's crucifixion, his burial in a sepulchre, the three days of darkness following his death, and the redemption that was to be wrought through his death.

That I might more fully persuade them to believe in the Lord
their Redeemer I did read unto them that which was written by
the prophet Isaiah; for I did liken all scriptures unto us,
that it might be for our profit and learning.

1 NEPHI 19:23

Spiritual strength comes to those who sincerely
study the scriptures. Nephi understood the power of
scripture and wanted to share its influence with his
brothers. He taught them from the writings of Isaiah
for the purpose of teaching and testifying of Christ—
the scriptural message of greatest worth. Scripture
study and gospel teaching bring people to Christ and
make timeless principles timely. Nephi applied Isaiah's
writing to his own family, not just to the house of
Israel. We can do the same. As we read, study, and
ponder holy writ, we can ask ourselves, *What does this*
scripture mean to me and to my family today? How can I apply this
message to my life? Why is this passage included in such a relatively
short text? These and other questions can open our
minds and hearts to the everlasting truths of Jesus
Christ.

Behold, I have refined thee,
I have chosen thee in the furnace of affliction.

1 NEPHI 20:10

Followers of Christ in all dispensations are no strangers to sorrow. They know pain and are well acquainted with affliction. The crucible of life gives us opportunities to become better or bitter, refined or rebellious, submissive or stiff-necked. The tempered steel of faith is forged in the flames of suffering. Ease does not call forth greatness or strength of commitment. When the fires of sickness, failure, disappointment, and even tragedy engulf us, if we are spiritually prepared, God's peace can carry us through safely. That doesn't mean we try to ignore the heartache or deny the reality of the pain. Rather, we take an authentic look at it, enlarging our perspective by believing that some good can come from crucible experiences. When they come— as they surely will—we can rise above them by setting our hearts on everlasting things. Isaiah promised, "They that wait upon the Lord shall renew their strength; they shall mount up with wings as eagles" (Isaiah 40:31).

It is a light thing that thou shouldst be my servant to raise up the tribes of Jacob, and to restore the preserved of Israel. I will also give thee for a light to the Gentiles, that thou mayest be my salvation unto the ends of the earth.

1 NEPHI 21:6

Jehovah explained to ancient Israel that it is a "light thing" for them to maintain gospel standards among themselves. That is, it is not enough, not sufficient for them to keep the light of truth from others of our Father's children; the house of Israel is called upon to be a light to the world, to bring the message of the one true God and his plan of salvation to every nation, kindred, tongue, and people. In our own day Jehovah has spoken: "Therefore blessed are ye if ye continue in my goodness, a light unto the Gentiles, and through this priesthood, a savior unto my people Israel" (D&C 86:11).

Can a woman forget her sucking child, that she should not have compassion on the son of her womb? Yea, they may forget, yet will I not forget thee, O house of Israel. Behold, I have graven thee upon the palms of my hands.

1 NEPHI 21:15–16

The Good Shepherd has promised to comfort his people. While in a time of crisis an otherwise loving mother might be tempted to abandon the child of her womb, the God of Israel will never forget the children of his covenant, the house of Israel. Those who make and keep sacred covenants can be assured that the Lord will not leave them comfortless. The imagery Nephi used to describe this covenant relationship alludes to the ancient practice of tattooing the palms of individuals' hands with a symbol of the temple or other sacred emblem to show devotion and to serve as a reminder of their holy commitments. Similarly, the wounds of the Crucifixion keep our Lord ever mindful of those for whom he gave his life. These images of blood and pain make clear the depth and breadth of his love for us. He will ever remember those who come unto him. Our part is to "always remember him, and keep his commandments" (Moroni 4:3).

The house of Israel . . . will be scattered upon all the face of the earth, and also among all nations. . . . they are scattered to and fro upon the isles of the sea; and whither they are none of us knoweth.

1 NEPHI 22:3–4

Since the time of Joseph Smith there has been much speculation about the gathering of the ten tribes, those descendants of Jacob (Israel) who were taken captive by the Assyrians in 721 B.C. and became lost to the knowledge of the world. Nephi explained that the ten tribes are scattered among the nations, as lost to their own identity as they are to their geography. They are being gathered in the same way as anyone else is gathered—by hearing the message of the restored gospel, accepting its principles and precepts, being baptized at the hands of authorized servants, and congregating with those of the true church. Thus, the great work of gathering is brought to pass through missionary work. Though remnants of the lost tribes are even now coming into the Church, the great day of the gathering of the ten tribes lies ahead, in the Millennium (3 Nephi 21:24–26).

The time cometh that after all the house of Israel have been scattered and confounded, that the Lord God will raise up a mighty nation among the Gentiles, yea, even upon the face of this land; and by them shall our seed be scattered.

1 Nephi 22:7

From Nephi's perspective there were only two types of people—Jews and Gentiles. The descendants of Lehi were Jews because they had come out of the land of Jerusalem (2 Nephi 30:4; 33:8). All others from other lands, including those who were lineal descendants of Abraham, Isaac, and Jacob, were identified as Gentiles (D&C 109:60). Nephi thus spoke prophetically of the establishment of the kingdom of God in a great Gentile nation under the direction of a great Gentile prophet. The delivery by the Gentiles of the gospel to the Jews and the descendants of Lehi is likened to the latter groups being invited to the royal gospel banquet and treated as royalty.

*The day soon cometh that all the proud
and they who do wickedly shall be as stubble.*

1 Nephi 22:15

Satan, who is the god of this world (2 Corinthians 4:4), is alive and well on planet Earth; truly, it is the day of his power, "for we wrestle not against flesh and blood, but against principalities, against powers, against the rulers of the darkness of this world, against spiritual wickedness in high places" (Ephesians 6:12). But one day all of that will change. The God of heaven will step into history once again, bring an end to worldwide wickedness, and initiate a thousand years of peace and righteousness. In short, the Millennium will be brought in by power, and it will be maintained by the righteousness of the people. The righteous "shall not be hewn down and cast into the fire, but shall abide the day. And the earth shall be given unto them for an inheritance; and they shall multiply and wax strong, and their children shall grow up without sin unto salvation" (D&C 45:57–58).

A prophet shall the Lord your God raise up unto you, like unto me [Moses]; him shall ye hear in all things whatsoever he shall say unto you. And it shall come to pass that all those who will not hear that prophet shall be cut off from among the people.

1 NEPHI 22:20

The Lord has declared that "he that receiveth my servants receiveth me" (D&C 84:36). Conversely, he that rejects the servants of the Lord rejects that Lord who sent them. In 1 Nephi 22:20 Nephi affirms the prophecy in Deuteronomy 18:15–19 concerning the coming of the Savior and warns that those who will not hear "that prophet" (Jesus) will be cut off from among the people of the covenant. The risen Lord applied the same principle and warning to those who choose to reject his anointed servants. Speaking of the Prophet Joseph Smith, the Savior declared that "whosoever will not believe in my words, who am Jesus Christ, which the Father shall cause him to bring forth unto the Gentiles, and shall give unto him power that he shall bring them forth unto the Gentiles, (it shall be done even as Moses said) they shall be cut off from among my people who are of the covenant" (3 Nephi 21:11).

Awake! and arise from the dust, and hear the words of a trembling parent, whose limbs ye must soon lay down in the cold and silent grave.

2 NEPHI 1:14

What faithful parents have not prayed and pleaded with the Lord to bless their children? What dedicated parents have not been "weighed down with sorrow from time to time," fearing for the eternal welfare of a son or daughter? (2 Nephi 1:17). All good parents encourage their children to "put on the armor of righteousness" and "shake off the chains with which [they] are bound" (2 Nephi 1:23). Knowing his own death was imminent, Lehi exhorted his children to undergo a spiritual rebirth. He implored his family to awake from the deep sleep of apathy and wickedness; he urged them to be united and determined in following the gospel path; he commanded them to rebel no more against righteous models and murmur no more against the power of God (2 Nephi 1:13–32). Devoted fathers and mothers "have no greater joy than to hear that [their] children walk in truth" (3 John 1:4). As an individual and as a parent, Lehi endured faithful to the end.

The Lord hath redeemed my soul from hell; I have beheld his glory, and I am encircled about eternally in the arms of his love.

2 NEPHI 1:15

Having served God all his days, Lehi, now in the twilight of his life, confidently declared himself redeemed from hell. That is, through his faithfulness he became free from the blood and sins of his generation. His eternal salvation was assured. Lehi first beheld the glory of Jesus Christ before he and his family even left Jerusalem (1 Nephi 1:6–12). He and his family had experienced much since then, but his witness only grew stronger. Lehi used the present tense to describe his being encircled in the arms of the Lord's love—he did not say *I will be* (at some future date) *encircled,* but *I am encircled.* We too can live with such faithfulness and devotion that we feel encircled in the arms of the Savior's love. That does not mean we are perfect; nor does it mean we will not have our share of heartache and sorrow. It does mean, however, that as we continually and sincerely strive to do his will, we will walk in his love and light.

*Thou art redeemed, because of the righteousness of thy Redeemer.
. . . wherefore, thou art blessed even as they unto whom he shall
minister in the flesh; for the Spirit is the same, yesterday,
today, and forever. And the way is prepared from the
fall of man, and salvation is free.*

2 NEPHI 2:3–4

The gospel of Jesus Christ is a covenant, a two-way promise. It sets forth those things that God does for us that we cannot do for ourselves: forgive our sins, cleanse our hearts, change our nature, raise us from the dead, and glorify us hereafter. For our part, we agree to do the things that we can do: have faith in Christ, repent of our sins, be baptized at the hands of a legal administrator, receive the gift of the Holy Ghost, and endure faithfully to the end of our lives. Our human works, our good works, are necessary but insufficient to save us. Foundational to the covenant is the love of God the Father and the perfect righteousness of his Son Jesus Christ. The Mediator stands before the Father and pleads our cause, not on the basis of our paltry deeds, but on the basis of his merits, his sacrifice, suffering, death, and resurrection (D&C 45:3–5).

Men are instructed sufficiently that they know good from evil.
And the law is given unto men. And by the law no flesh is
justified. . . . Yea, by the temporal law they were cut off; and also,
by the spiritual law they perish from that which is good,
and become miserable forever.

2 NEPHI 2:5

Each of us is born with the light of Christ, which teaches us what is right and what is wrong, yet each of us, at one time or another, yields to the enticements of the world and thus becomes guilty of sin. We thereby disqualify ourselves from entrance into the presence of God, for no unclean thing can dwell in his presence. When both Lehi and Paul declared that by the law no flesh is justified (2 Nephi 2:5; Romans 3:20), they taught that no person, not even the greatest prophet, traverses life's paths without yielding to sin. Not one of us can be justified (declared clean, made righteous) by works or by law. Jesus alone never sinned nor took a spiritual detour. Our only hope for peace here and salvation hereafter is to rely upon and hold tenaciously to the One who has lived the law perfectly and therefore owes no debt to justice. Our only hope is to be justified through faith in Christ.

*Behold, he offereth himself a sacrifice for sin,
to answer the ends of the law, unto all those who have
a broken heart and a contrite spirit; and unto none
else can the ends of the law be answered.*

2 NEPHI 2:7

The Lord asks us to repent of our sins and come unto him with a broken heart and a contrite spirit (3 Nephi 12:19). To be broken and contrite means to be humble, to feel godly sorrow for sin, to know that without heaven's help we are lost. When we feel broken, we want to be healed, yet we cannot heal ourselves. True peace and lasting happiness come through our Savior, who offered himself as a sacrifice for sin, fulfilled the ends of the law, and gave his life that we might live. The great Healer comforts our souls as we come unto him in humility and complete submission. Nephi's plea resounds in our hearts: "May the gates of hell be shut continually before me, because that my heart is broken and my spirit is contrite" (2 Nephi 4:32). With broken hearts and contrite spirits, because we need to be healed and made whole, we come to our great Redeemer in gratitude and rejoicing.

How great the importance to make these things known unto the inhabitants of the earth, that they may know that there is no flesh that can dwell in the presence of God, save it be through the merits, and mercy, and grace of the Holy Messiah.

2 NEPHI 2:8

I t is infinitely important that parents teach their children the principles and doctrines that will prepare them to choose eternal life (D&C 68:25–28; 93:40). Fundamental to such teaching is the doctrine of Christ, the message that "salvation was, and is, and is to come, in and through the atoning blood of Christ, the Lord Omnipotent" (Mosiah 3:18). Children need to understand that Jesus Christ "hath abolished death, and hath brought life and immortality to light through the gospel" (2 Timothy 1:10). No amount of formal education or training in the finest universities of the world will compensate for the lack of such teaching. Thus, in the words of Jacob, "Why not speak of the atonement of Christ?" (Jacob 4:12). Similarly, Nephi taught that "we talk of Christ, we rejoice in Christ, we preach of Christ . . . that our children may know to what source they may look for a remission of their sins" (2 Nephi 25:26).

It must needs be, that there is an opposition in all things.
If not so, . . . righteousness could not be brought to pass, neither
wickedness, neither holiness nor misery, neither good nor bad.
Wherefore, all things must needs be a compound in one.

2 NEPHI 2:11

Imagine a world in which all things were the same:
no contrast of color, function, shape, or size. We
couldn't really love because we would not understand
hate or even dislike. Without sorrow we would not
know joy; without pain we could not appreciate peace
and comfort; without darkness we could not have
light. And though it might appear enticing to live in a
world with no sadness, no malice or heartache, that
experience would not teach us, stretch us, and develop
within us the attributes of godliness. No virtue can
exist without its corresponding evil. No agency can
exist without choice. Wickedness must be so that
there might be righteousness, death so that there
might be life. We are here to comprehend that everything has its opposite, to gain experience through the
vicissitudes of life, and exercise our agency to *choose* the
right.

*If ye shall say there is no law, ye shall also say there is no sin. If ye
shall say there is no sin, ye shall also say there is no righteousness.
. . . And if these things are not there is no God.*

2 NEPHI 2:13

The Father's gracious plan of happiness grants us
the capacity to choose. But for agency to operate, there
must be law, knowledge, and choices. Without opposition,
without agency, mortal life would be without
meaning or purpose. Laws are essential to learning and
progress. Good could not be defined without evil. Any
philosophy that tries to free us from guilt by teaching
there is no law, no sin, and no unrighteousness leads
directly to an argument for the nonexistence of God.
It is an approach as old as time, as deadly as ever, and it
is always promoted by the father of lies (Helaman
13:26–28). God allows us to choose life or death, happiness
or misery (Helaman 14:30–31). He will not
force us to be good, and the devil cannot compel us to
do evil. Each day we can decide to follow God's plan
and his laws, walking in the way of happiness and eternal
life.

Adam fell that men might be; and men are,
that they might have joy.

2 NEPHI 2:25

In partaking of the fruit of the tree of knowledge of good and evil, Adam obeyed the Father's other great commandment to have posterity. By so doing, Adam and Eve were the means for introducing death into the world: temporal death, or separation of body and spirit; and spiritual death, or separation from God and his angels (Moses 6:48). Christ came to redeem us from the Fall, to make us free forever if we follow him and do his will (2 Nephi 2:26). The Fall also makes everlasting joy and happiness possible, redeeming us from the woes of this world. Mother Eve perfectly expressed the doctrine of the Fall: "Were it not for our transgression we never should have had seed, and never should have known good and evil, and the joy of our redemption, and the eternal life which God giveth unto all the obedient" (Moses 5:11). Because we experience sorrow in this life, we can experience and appreciate joy both here and hereafter.

*Messiah cometh . . . that he may redeem the children of men
from the fall. And because that they are redeemed from the fall
they have become free forever, knowing good from evil;
to act for themselves and not to be acted upon,
save it be by the punishment of the law.*

2 NEPHI 2:26

The Fall and the Atonement are a package deal. Indeed, "just as man does not really desire food until he is hungry, so he does not desire the salvation of Christ until he knows why he needs Christ," said President Ezra Taft Benson. "No one adequately and properly knows why he needs Christ until he understands and accepts the doctrine of the Fall and its effect upon all mankind" (*Witness and a Warning,* 33). Moroni declared that "by Adam came the fall of man. And because of the fall of man came Jesus Christ, even the Father and the Son; and because of Jesus Christ came the redemption of man" (Mormon 9:12). When we begin to realize the breadth and depth of the Fall, we begin to sense how desperately we need divine help. We then can see that Jesus is much more than a spiritual adviser or a special friend. He is our Savior and Redeemer, our only hope.

Men are free according to the flesh; and all things are given them
which are expedient unto man. And they are free to choose
liberty and eternal life, through the great Mediator of all men,
or to choose captivity and death, according to the
captivity and power of the devil.

2 NEPHI 2:27

Agency is freedom of the soul, the unfettered right to choose. It is essential to the plan of salvation. Righteousness cannot be forced because, as Lehi taught, if there is no opportunity for wickedness, there can be no opportunity for righteousness (2 Nephi 10:23). What could righteousness possibly mean if it were forced upon us? The attributes of godliness are developed only when coupled with the ability to choose. The Savior's redeeming sacrifice grants us the opportunity for eternal life—but only if we choose to follow him. The righteous followers of Christ cleave unto that which is "honest, true, chaste, benevolent . . . virtuous, lovely, or of good report or praiseworthy" (Article of Faith 13); whereas the companions of evil seek for that which is foolish, false, carnal, sensual, and devilish. That which is of Satan debases. That which is of God exalts and purifies. This is the day to freely and wholly choose the Lord and his righteousness.

A choice seer will I raise up out of the fruit of thy loins; . . . and unto him will I give power to bring forth my word unto the seed of thy loins . . . to the convincing them of my word, which shall have already gone forth among them.

2 NEPHI 3:7, 11

Among the plain and precious truths lost before our present Bible was compiled are the marvelous prophecies of Joseph, the son of Jacob who was sold into Egypt. Nephi explained that "the prophecies which [Joseph] wrote, there are not many greater" (2 Nephi 4:2). In speaking to his youngest son, Joseph, Lehi drew upon a more extensive prophecy of Joseph of Egypt now found only in the Joseph Smith Translation of Genesis 50. Lehi taught his son Joseph about a "choice seer," a man raised up in the last days, of the lineage of Joseph of old, who would serve a vital role in restoring plain and precious truths and once again establishing the everlasting covenant on earth. In addition, that choice seer—clearly, Joseph Smith—would bring forth the word of God that would convince latter-day readers of the essential truthfulness of the Bible; in short, the Book of Mormon would prove to the world that the holy scriptures are true (D&C 20:11).

That which shall be written by the fruit of thy loins, and also that which shall be written by the fruit of the loins of Judah, shall grow together, unto the confounding of false doctrines . . . and bringing them . . . to the knowledge of my covenants.

2 NEPHI 3:12

The greatest commentary on scripture is scripture itself. The more familiar we are with ancient scripture, for example, the more we appreciate the power and clarity of latter-day scripture. Likewise, when we have become more than distant acquaintances with latter-day scripture, we are in a position to recognize pearls of great price within the records of antiquity. In this verse we are given an awesome promise: through joining the Book of Mormon to the Bible, studying them together, and thus expounding all the scriptures in one (Luke 24:27; 3 Nephi 23:14), the door will be open for the receipt of truth, the dissipation of error, and an endowment of light and understanding.

*O wretched man that I am! Yea, my heart sorroweth because of
my flesh; my soul grieveth because of mine iniquities.
I am encompassed about, because of the temptations and the sins
which do so easily beset me. . . . nevertheless,
I know in whom I have trusted.*

2 NEPHI 4:17–19

It is hard to imagine Nephi as a "wretched man."
Most of us would give anything to be as wretched as
he was! Yet in his exclamation of unworthiness, we see
the effect of the Spirit of the Lord upon an already
softened heart, the influence of the Comforter, working through the light of Christ, to heighten sensitivity
to the slightest sins. It was only because Nephi was as
pure as he was that he was able to discern those elements of his nature, few though they may have been,
that were not in complete harmony with the divine
will. At the same time Nephi provides for us the formula for his own and our success in life: While he
acknowledged freely his weakness, he knew fully the
source of his strength. His trust was not in himself but
rather in an all-powerful, all-knowing, and all-loving
God.

*O Lord, I have trusted in thee, and I will trust in thee
forever. . . . yea, I will cry unto thee, my God,
the rock of my righteousness.*

2 NEPHI 4:34–35

Because all of us are less than perfect, even the best
of men and women can let us down and disappoint us
from time to time. If we rely on the many impressive
people and things of this world, they can all fall short,
get us off track, or even worse, lead us astray. But if we
put our complete trust in Jesus, the One who is perfect and beyond reproach, we find salvation. He is the
Rock of our righteousness and the Source of our salvation. He who is whole can heal those who are broken. He who is perfect can teach and inspire us who
are imperfect. He who is love personified can comfort
our souls and whisper peace to troubled hearts. "Trust
in the Lord with all thine heart; and lean not unto
thine own understanding. In all thy ways acknowledge
him, and he shall direct thy paths" (Proverbs 3:5–6).
Our trust, our faith, our hope must center in the
Savior.

We did observe to keep the judgments, and the statutes,
and the commandments of the Lord in all things,
according to the law of Moses.
2 NEPHI 5:10

It may be difficult to understand completely what
the Book of Mormon means by saying the Nephites
kept the law of Moses. In a way, because they had the
higher priesthood and the fulness of the gospel, the
law had become dead to them, for they were "made
alive in Christ because of [their] faith" (2 Nephi
25:25). Elder Bruce R. McConkie wrote: "The
Nephites offered sacrifices and kept the law of Moses.
Since they held the Melchizedek priesthood and there
were no Levites among them, we suppose their sacrifices were those that antedated the ministry of Moses
and . . . they kept the law of Moses in the sense that
they conformed to its myriad moral principles. . . .
There is, at least, no intimation in the Book of
Mormon that the Nephites offered the daily sacrifices
. . . or that they held the various feasts that were part
of the religious life of their Old World kinsmen"
(*Promised Messiah*, 427).

I, Nephi, did build a temple; and I did construct it after the manner of the temple of Solomon save it were not built of so many precious things; for they were not to be found upon the land. . . . But . . . the workmanship thereof was exceedingly fine.

2 NEPHI 5:16

The Lord's people have always been a temple-building people. Indeed, the temple was the focal point of true religion, the sacred ground ordained as the meeting place between God and man, the house of revelation, and the place of eternal covenants. It is commonly held by the Jews that there can be but one temple—the temple in Jerusalem. Scripture testifies otherwise. A covenant-centered religion requires a covenant sanctuary. The fact that the Nephites constructed a temple suggests the possibility that many of the remnants of Israel, wherever they have been scattered, would have done likewise, if they possessed the holy priesthood (D&C 124:39; see Abraham, facsimile 2, explanation of figure 3).

He had caused the cursing to come upon them, yea, even a sore cursing, because of their iniquity. For behold, they had hardened their hearts against him, that they had become like unto a flint.

2 Nephi 5:21

Alma taught that we bring upon ourselves the curse or condemnation of God through our own unfaithfulness (Alma 3:19). Once the Lamanites had broken from the Nephites, once they had begun to deny the teachings and righteous traditions they had been given, and once they had turned from the God of Abraham, Isaac and Jacob, they forfeited the right to the Spirit of the Lord and wandered in darkness. Thus the curse upon the Lamanites was a loss of the blessings of heaven. Later in our story, at the time of Samuel the Lamanite, the Nephites fell into sustained wickedness and thus opened themselves to a similar cursing. Samuel reminded the Nephites that "whosoever perisheth, perisheth unto himself; and whosoever doeth iniquity, doeth it unto himself; for behold, ye are free; ye are permitted to act for yourselves" (Helaman 14:30).

It came to pass that we lived after the manner of happiness.
2 NEPHI 5:27

The Prophet Joseph Smith taught that "happiness is the object and design of our existence; and will be the end thereof, if we pursue the path that leads to it; and this path is virtue, uprightness, faithfulness, holiness, and keeping all the commandments of God" (*Teachings*, 255–56.) In many ways, happiness is a byproduct, not just an end product, of faithful living. Happiness will generally be found in the journey as well as in the destination and may or may not be related to the conditions in which we find themselves. At this stage of Nephite history, the covenant people were frequently involved in conflict and warfare, facing staggering obstacles to simply maintain their freedoms and liberties. But they were happy, content in life because they enjoyed the quiet affirmation of the Spirit that the Lord was pleased with them. In short, happiness comes as a fruit of the Spirit, not as a result of worldly applause or accomplishment.

Nevertheless, I speak unto you again; for I am desirous for the welfare of your souls. Yea, mine anxiety is great for you; and ye yourselves know that it ever has been.

2 NEPHI 6:3

Jacob, the son of Lehi, used the words *anxious* or *anxiety* more often than did any other speaker or writer in the Book of Mormon. He loved the Nephites. He loved his brethren, the Lamanites. And he loved those who would receive his words in a future day. Because he cared so deeply about all those people, he especially desired that they truly hear the message of salvation and internalize it, repent of their sins, and turn to the Holy One of Israel for strength and support. As the Prophet Joseph Smith taught, "A man filled with the love of God, is not content with blessing his family alone, but ranges through the whole world, anxious to bless the whole human race" (*Teachings*, 174). Jacob's anxiety was not the kind that stifles or immobilizes but rather the kind that inspires and motivates to righteousness and diligence (Jacob 1:19).

*After they have hardened their hearts and stiffened their necks
against the Holy One of Israel, behold, the judgments of the Holy
One of Israel shall come upon them. And the day cometh that
they shall be smitten and afflicted.*

2 NEPHI 6:10

The sins of the fathers and mothers are visited upon the heads of their children and grandchildren to the extent that the children and grandchildren individually choose to follow the same course their forebears chose. Because we know that "men will be punished for their own sins and not for Adam's transgression" (Article of Faith 2), we also know that no one will be held responsible for what their ancestors have done. Any person who makes the choice to come out of darkness into the marvelous light of Christ leaves his scattered condition and is gathered to the Redeemer and his covenant people.

APRIL

*The bands of death shall be
broken, and the Son reigneth, and
hath power over the dead;
therefore, he bringeth to pass the
resurrection of the dead.*

MOSIAH 15:20

*Thus saith the Lord: Where is the bill of your mother's
divorcement? To whom have I put thee away, or to which
of my creditors have I sold you? . . . Behold, for your
iniquities have ye sold yourselves, and for your
transgressions is your mother put away.*

2 NEPHI 7:1

To redeem is to purchase or buy back. When we
sin, we essentially sell ourselves to the devil, for we sell
ourselves short of all we could be. As we come unto
Christ by covenant, our Divine Redeemer offers to
purchase us, to buy us back, to reclaim us, to reinstate
us in the royal family. Thus the worth of souls is great
(D&C 18:10), not just because we are sons and daughters of God and have unlimited eternal possibilities
but because an infinite price has been paid for us, a
price that entailed the shedding of the blood of an
infinite Being. Paul taught, "Know ye not that your
body is the temple of the Holy Ghost which is in you,
which ye have of God, and ye are not your own? For
ye are bought with a price" (1 Corinthians 6:19–20).

Lift up your eyes to the heavens, and look upon the earth beneath;
for the heavens shall vanish away like smoke, and the earth shall
wax old like a garment; and they that dwell therein shall die
in like manner. But my salvation shall be forever,
and my righteousness shall not be abolished.

2 NEPHI 8:6

We search the scriptures, we ponder upon the holy word to come to know our God—who he is, what he has done, what he is now doing, and what he will yet do for those who come unto him. Through the scriptures we learn of God's constancy. He is everlastingly the same and may be relied upon to fulfill his word according to his promises. God is God, and his position as the Supreme Governor of the universe is forever fixed; he will not apostatize from exaltation, nor will the blessings of salvation promised to the faithful be lost to those who qualify for them. In short, we look to God with confidence and assurance, acknowledging that "though the heavens and the earth pass away, [his] word shall not pass away, but shall all be fulfilled" (D&C 1:38).

*To fulfil the merciful plan of the great Creator, there must needs
be a power of resurrection, and the resurrection must needs
come unto man by reason of the fall; and the fall came by
reason of transgression; and because man became fallen
they were cut off from the presence of the Lord.*

2 NEPHI 9:6

In a sense, we die as to premortality in order to be
born into mortality. Likewise, we must die as pertaining to time in order to be born into eternity. The separation of the physical body and the eternal spirit is a
necessary part of the plan of God, for, as Alma
explained, to reclaim man from this temporal death
would destroy the great plan of happiness (Alma
42:8). Truly, death passes upon all men and women to
fulfil "the merciful plan of the great Creator" (2 Nephi
9:6). It is merciful in the sense that it delivers us from
the toils and agonies of this life. "When men are prepared," the Prophet Joseph Smith observed, "they are
better off to go hence" (*Teachings,* 326). Death is merciful too because it opens us to a new phase of life, a
time wherein the restrictions of our mortal tabernacles are gone and the spirit can soar.

O the wisdom of God, his mercy and grace! For behold, if the flesh
should rise no more our spirits must become subject to that
angel who fell from before the presence of the Eternal God,
and became the devil, to rise no more.

2 NEPHI 9:8

T he revelations attest that no one may be saved in the highest heaven without divine assistance and that the highest degree of the celestial kingdom comes only to those who are valiant in the testimony of Jesus. One sin on our part disqualifies us from salvation, inasmuch as we have no way of procuring forgiveness and reinstatement on our own. Further, the resurrection of Jesus Christ is the tangible evidence that he was who he said he was and that he could do what he said he could do: raise us from the dead and forgive our sins. If Jesus did not rise from the tomb (as he said he would), how can we trust that he can forgive our sins (as he said he could)? If there were no resurrection, there would be no atonement, and all of us would be lost forever.

O how great the holiness of our God! For he knoweth all things,
and there is not anything save he knows it.

2 NEPHI 9:20

The Prophet Joseph Smith taught that it is impossible for any rational and intelligent being to exercise faith unto life and salvation in a being who does not possess all of the attributes of godliness in perfection. He explained that "without the knowledge of all things, God would not be able to save any portion of his creatures; . . . and if it were not for the idea existing in the minds of men that God had all knowledge it would be impossible for them to exercise faith in him" (*Lectures on Faith* 4:11). We can rest confident in the knowledge that there is no question we may pose that will stump our Heavenly Father, no personal challenge about which we cannot receive divine direction, no eternal truth of which he is ignorant. Our God is God, and he knows all things.

He cometh into the world that he may save all men if they will hearken unto his voice; for behold, he suffereth the pains of all men, yea, the pains of every living creature, both men, women, and children, who belong to the family of Adam.

2 NEPHI 9:21

It is not uncommon to hear the teaching that Jesus suffered only for those who choose to repent of their sins and come unto him. Yet the scriptures, ancient and modern, teach otherwise. Although it is true that forgiveness and restoration come only to the penitent, our Master suffered in Gethsemane and on Golgotha for all men and women. This is why ignoring or spurning his gentle, godly offer is in truth a mockery and a refusal of the most significant gift in all time and eternity. Jesus "suffered the pain of all men, that all men might repent and come unto him" (D&C 18:11; see also 19:16). "For what doth it profit a man if a gift is bestowed upon him, and he receive not the gift? Behold, he rejoices not in that which is given unto him, neither rejoices in him who is the giver of the gift" (D&C 88:33).

*He commandeth all men that they must repent, and be baptized
in his name, having perfect faith in the Holy One of Israel,
or they cannot be saved in the kingdom of God.*

2 NEPHI 9:23

Jacob presented the astounding and frightening truth that only those who exercise "perfect faith" in the Holy One of Israel can be saved in the kingdom of God. Perfect faith. Perfect faith! Who do you know that has perfect faith? It appears that Jacob taught the simple yet profound reality that those who inherit the kingdom of God are those who have learned to trust completely, rely wholly, and have undeviating confidence in the atoning blood and enabling power of Jesus Christ. We exercise perfect faith in him through a thorough acknowledgment of his merits, mercy, and grace, and of our absolute ineptitude without him. Thus the great thrust in our lives should be not the quest for self-esteem but rather the acquisition of Christ-esteem; it is not self-confidence that will boost us into glory but complete confidence in him who lived the law perfectly that will both make up the difference and make all the difference.

He has given a law; and where there is no law given there is no punishment; and where there is no punishment there is no condemnation; and where there is no condemnation the mercies of the Holy One of Israel have claim upon them, because of the atonement.

2 NEPHI 9:25

Often we hear the comment, "That's not fair!" In fact, even those who walk by the light of faith in the restored gospel will encounter a myriad of situations that for the time being, at least, are simply not fair. Not every imbalance or inequity will be corrected in this life. Complete fairness will not come until the Lord's entire plan for the happiness of his children has been put into effect and the playing field of life has been leveled. But, more than being fair, our God is forevermore just and merciful. Thus, an unconditional benefit of the Atonement is that no one will be eternally disadvantaged for not living the gospel when he or she was ignorant of it, and no one will be punished for not receiving an ordinance that was not available.

*O the vainness, and the frailties, and the foolishness of men!
When they are learned they think they are wise, and they hearken
not unto the counsel of God. . . . And they shall perish. But to be
learned is good if they hearken unto the counsels of God.*

2 NEPHI 9:28–29

If is a word that changes everything. Education is good, even essential, *if* we hearken unto the counsels of God. Prophets have always encouraged us to study, to learn and ponder. But they've also cautioned us to be wise, for we may be "ever learning, and never able to come to the knowledge of the truth"—the truth that really matters (2 Timothy 3:7). Some may think that meek servants of the Lord who are preachers of righteousness don't understand very much about the universe and things in it. It has ever been so, because the devil would convince us that intellectualism is the pathway to peace and knowledge. In the end, what we know in our minds will be ever so meaningless if we don't know and feel the truths of the gospel in our hearts. The gifts of the Spirit that mightily change our hearts will bring us closer to the infinite truth of the everlasting God.

Whoso knocketh, to him will he open; and the wise, and the learned, and they that are rich, who are puffed up because of their learning, and their wisdom, and their riches— yea, . . . save they shall . . . come down in the depths of humility, he will not open unto them.

2 NEPHI 9:42

The Lord's door is always open to the faithful who are pure in thought and action. The faithful may or may not be the learned or the rich. The size of bank account or degree of education is not what matters before the Lord. He looks on the heart and stands ready to bless (Matthew 6:19–21). But those who are puffed up with pride because of their money, education, and their supposed wisdom will be closed everlastingly to the Lord's love and light. The apostle Peter taught: "Be clothed with humility: for God resisteth the proud, and giveth grace to the humble. Humble yourselves therefore under the mighty hand of God, that he may exalt you in due time" (1 Peter 5:5–6). The things of this world—the possessions, prestige, and positions we have—will all soon pass away. But the things of eternity live forever.

Do not spend money for that which is of no worth, nor your labor for that which cannot satisfy. . . . come unto the Holy One of Israel, and feast upon that which perisheth not, neither can be corrupted. . . . Let your hearts rejoice.

2 NEPHI 9:51–52

Few things stand the test of time. A latest, greatest innovation or idea is always on the horizon. But rising above the mad dash for the newfangled is the message of the everlasting gospel: Our Father in Heaven so loved us that he sent his Only Begotten Son to ransom us from sin and death. Our beloved Savior gave his life for us that we may be forgiven and, if we are true and faithful, inherit all that the Father hath. These are the words of eternity. This is the feast that does not perish, the bread of life that daily sustains us (John 6:35–48). We can be spiritually fed and lifted by the Lord's grace—every day. When we are discouraged, he lifts us with his radiant life. When we feel alone and afraid, he beckons us to come unto him. These things will never change; they are the immutable, ineffable truths of the great plan of happiness. May our hearts rejoice in them.

Behold, the Lord God has led away from time to time from the house of Israel, according to his will and pleasure. And now behold, the Lord remembereth all them who have been broken off, wherefore he remembereth us also.

2 NEPHI 10:22

Generally speaking, Israel is scattered when they reject the true Messiah and his gospel, when they turn to the worship of false gods or spurn the redemption of the Holy One of Israel. There is, however, another reason that the people of Israel are scattered: to allow the descendants of Abraham to be spread far and wide, to enable those with believing blood to become a leavening influence. One of the promises made to the fathers is that the descendants of Abraham, Isaac, and Jacob would be found throughout the earth to provide an influence for good among all of our Father's children. Thus, "when the most High divided to the nations their inheritance, when he separated the sons of Adam, he set the bounds of the people according to the number of the children of Israel. For the Lord's portion is his people; Jacob is the lot of his inheritance" (Deuteronomy 32:8–9).

Cheer up your hearts, and remember that ye are free to act for yourselves—to choose the way of everlasting death or the way of eternal life.

2 NEPHI 10:23

Being tempted by evil is as essential to agency as being led by the Spirit of God (D&C 29:39), else what could our choices mean? The great plan of happiness ensures that no one is forced to choose—either righteousness or wickedness. We are free to do whatever we choose. "God would not exert any compulsory means, and the devil could not," taught the Prophet Joseph (*Teachings,* 187). Each day we make choices that give us more freedom, opportunity, and blessing, or we act in a way that limits heaven's beneficence and increases our bondage. The great paradox is that as we wholly surrender our will to God's, we become free and gain complete victory. We develop the attributes of godliness by our freewill choices that are pure and holy. Indeed, the gift of agency is one of God's greatest endowments to us. Only with agency can we, without compulsion or manipulation, become like God.

*Wherefore, my beloved brethren, reconcile yourselves to the will
of God, and not to the will of the devil and the flesh; and
remember, after ye are reconciled unto God, that it is
only in and through the grace of God that ye are saved.*

2 NEPHI 10:24

M en and women who have come to the gospel
covenant open themselves to spiritual graces more and
more as they learn to reconcile themselves to the will
of God. One of the lessons of a lifetime is that God
knows far better what to do with us than we do, and
to the extent that we yield our hearts unto him
(Helaman 3:35; D&C 88:67–68), we realize our full
potential in life and find great satisfaction and fulfillment in doing so. Moroni thus declared, on the last
page of the Book of Mormon, that as we deny ourselves of ungodliness and love God with all of our soul,
"then is his grace sufficient for you, that by his grace
ye may be perfect in Christ" (Moroni 10:32).

I, Nephi, write more of the words of Isaiah. . . . for he verily saw
my Redeemer, even as I have seen him. And my brother, Jacob,
also has seen him as I have seen him. . . . Wherefore, by the words
of three, God hath said, I will establish my word.

2 NEPHI 11:2–3

All gospel truths must be established in the mouth of multiple witnesses. This principle is replete throughout the Book of Mormon. In fact, the book itself is another witness of Jesus Christ (2 Nephi 29:8). In Lehi's family, Lehi, Nephi, and Jacob all testify of Christ, as does their prophet predecessor Isaiah (1 Nephi 12:6; 2 Nephi 2:3–4; Isaiah 6:1). Nephi, and later Mormon, went to great effort to see that Isaiah's witness of Christ was included in the small plates. Isaiah's words, written only 100 to 150 years before the days of Nephi, would have been viewed by the Nephites much as we view the sermons of Joseph Smith. They were cherished and handed down with great care. They are meant to be pondered and understood, not skipped over or hurried through. As did Nephi of old, we, too, will delight in the words of Isaiah as we make space for them in our hearts and minds.

My soul delighteth in proving unto my people the truth of the coming of Christ; for, for this end hath the law of Moses been given; and all things which have been given of God from the beginning of the world, unto man, are the typifying of him.

2 NEPHI 11:4

No man or woman who is filled with the testimony of Jesus can rest while there are others in the world who do not know or experience the great blessings of the Atonement in their lives. People who are truly converted, like the sons of Mosiah, are "desirous that salvation should be declared to every creature, for they [cannot] bear that any human soul should perish" (Mosiah 28:3). And those who seek to strengthen their witness of the Savior begin to see him in all things—not only to recognize his hand in all things but also to acknowledge that all things, spiritual and temporal, bear record of him (Moses 6:63). "It is wholesome and proper to look for similitudes of Christ everywhere," Elder Bruce R. McConkie wrote, "and to use them repeatedly in keeping him and his laws uppermost in our minds" (*Promised Messiah*, 453).

My soul delighteth in the covenants of the Lord which he hath
made to our fathers; yea, my soul delighteth in his grace,
and in his justice, and power, and mercy in the great
and eternal plan of deliverance from death.

2 NEPHI 11:5

The joyous spirit that fills our souls as we teach of Christ and his gospel is inexpressible. Nephi and all who likewise embrace the spirit of truth have much cause to rejoice. For in faith and "works of righteousness," we find "peace in this world, and eternal life in the world to come" (D&C 59:23). Nephi reasoned: If there were no Redeemer, then there could be no God, for there would be no justice; and if there were no God, there could be no creation (2 Nephi 11:6–7). Thus, all of God's creations testify of his existence. The emphatic testimony of the Book of Mormon is that Christ is God, the God of creation, the God of salvation, the God of the Old Testament. We, too, can experience the supernal spirit of truth as we read this sacred record and testify of its truthfulness.

*Therefore, my people are gone into captivity, because they have
no knowledge; and their honorable men are famished,
and their multitude dried up with thirst.*

2 NEPHI 15:13

One of Jehovah's repeated indictments against ancient Israel was that they had no knowledge of him: "My people are destroyed for lack of knowledge: because thou hast rejected knowledge, I will also reject thee" (Hosea 4:6). It is not that ancient Israel did not know of their God cognitively, could not speak of him intelligently, or could not set forth his attributes and qualities articulately. Rather, the knowledge of which the scriptures speak here is a special kind of knowledge, a close and intimate relationship that ought to exist between God and his covenant people. Thus, when God anciently or in our day has condemned his people for not knowing him (JST Matthew 7:33; Mosiah 26:24–27), he is saying that their lives are not in harmony with his will, that they are not cultivating his Spirit in their daily walk and talk, and they have not committed to nor sought what Paul called "the mind of Christ" (1 Corinthians 2:16).

*Wo unto them that call evil good, and good evil, that put
darkness for light, and light for darkness, that put
bitter for sweet, and sweet for bitter!*

2 NEPHI 15:20

King Mosiah warned that "if the time comes that
the voice of the people doth choose iniquity, then is
the time that the judgments of God will come upon
you" (Mosiah 29:27). A priceless blessing that the
Latter-day Saints enjoy is to be led by living apostles
and prophets, by seers and revelators who seek to
know and make known the mind and will of the Lord
for his kingdom today. These seers, chosen servants
who behold "things which [are] not visible to the natural eye" (Moses 6:36), affirm and reaffirm the
absolute truths that God would have all men and
women abide by. Morality cannot be determined by
social consensus; decency cannot be established by
how a particular generation feels about things at a
given time. It is thus incumbent upon every follower
of the Perfect One to seek the spirit of inspiration, to
pray that our desires may be educated, and to plead
that our consciences may be sharpened and enhanced.

He will lift up an ensign to the nations from far, . . . and behold,
they shall come with speed swiftly; none shall be weary nor
stumble among them. . . . their horses' hoofs shall be counted like
flint, and their wheels like a whirlwind, their roaring like a lion.

2 NEPHI 15:26, 28

The prophet Isaiah sought anciently to describe in the best words he possessed a latter-day event. He foresaw the establishment of the kingdom of God in the last days and the means by which people would gather to the stakes of Zion speedily. What he communicated was that in the last days, by means of modern transportation, people would gather to Salt Lake City or to other central gathering places, and such rapid gathering would be brought to pass by power. This is an example of a prophecy that we can understand to some extent because we live in the days in which the prophecy is being fulfilled (2 Nephi 25:7–8).

Therefore, the Lord himself shall give you a sign—
Behold, a virgin shall conceive, and shall bear a son,
and shall call his name Immanuel.

2 NEPHI 17:14

Isaiah's prophecy of Immanuel ("God is with us")
actually has a dual fulfillment. In about 700 B.C., Syria
and Israel were plotting to overthrow the kingdom of
Judah. King Ahaz in Judah contemplated asking
another neighbor, Assyria, for help. Isaiah delivered a
very simple, straightforward message to Ahaz: Be still.
Fear not. Do not enter into a confederation with a foreign nation. Trust God. The prophet then offered the
king a sign, the comforting assurance that before a
young pregnant woman could give birth to a child and
before that child could speak, "the riches of Damascus
and the spoil of Samaria shall be taken away before the
king of Assyria" (2 Nephi 18:4). That is, "Hold on.
Before long the Lord will deliver you from your enemies, for God is with us." Some seven centuries later,
the virgin Mary gave birth to the Son of God (Matthew
1:23), and the ancient prophecy found its perfect fulfillment, for, in very deed, God was with us.

There shall come forth a rod out of the stem of Jesse, and a branch shall grow out of his roots. And the Spirit of the Lord shall rest upon him, the spirit of wisdom and understanding, the spirit of counsel and might, the spirit of knowledge and of the fear of the Lord.

2 NEPHI 21:1–2

Like many of his prophetic colleagues, Isaiah foresaw the call and ministry of the Prophet Joseph Smith. By modern revelation we learn that the stem of Jesse is Christ and the rod and the root of Jesse are the choice seer, Joseph Smith. He was indeed "a descendant of Jesse, as well as of Joseph, unto whom rightly belongs the priesthood, and the keys of the kingdom, for an ensign, and for the gathering of [the Lord's] people in the last days" (D&C 113:6). Joseph Smith was chosen before the foundations of this world "to bring forth the word of God to the people, and receive the fulness of the keys and power of the Priesthood of the Son of God. The Lord had his eye upon him, and upon his father, and upon his father's father, and upon their progenitors" (Young, *Journal of Discourses,* 7:289).

How art thou fallen from heaven, O Lucifer, son of the
morning! . . . For thou hast said in thy heart: . . .
I will be like the Most High. Yet thou shalt be brought
down to hell, to the sides of the pit.

2 NEPHI 24:12–15

When the Son of Man returns in glory, he will cleanse the earth by fire, wickedness in all its forms will be removed, and Satan will be bound by the righteousness of the people for a thousand years (1 Nephi 22:26). The one who rejected the plan of the Father and sought the Father's throne in our first estate (Moses 4:1–4) will be stripped of his power over the souls of the children of men and placed in that bottomless pit where he may not deceive the nations for a long, long time (Revelation 20:1–3). And thus amid the rampant wickedness of the last days, we cry out with the Revelator, "Even so, come, Lord Jesus" (Revelation 22:20).

*Wherefore, hearken, O my people, . . . for because the words of
Isaiah are not plain unto you, nevertheless they are plain unto all
those that are filled with the spirit of prophecy. . . . behold, my
soul delighteth in plainness unto my people, that they may learn.*
2 NEPHI 25:4

Profound truths need not be packaged in difficult
and thus distracting language. Indeed, some of the
greatest teachers of all time have been those who have
been able to teach the mysteries of God in a manner
as to be understood by the little child or the recent
convert and to be deeply valued by the lifelong member of the Church. There is a simplicity that lies
beyond complexity, and the "teacher come from God"
(John 3:2) is one who strives to preach and teach, like
Nephi, with plainness. Such teaching is compre-
hended, applied, and remembered. Such teaching rep-
resents the "pleasing word of God, yea, the word
which healeth the wounded soul" (Jacob 2:8). Truly,
the things that matter most are the things that may be
articulated with the sweetest simplicity.

*When that day shall come that they . . . worship the Father in his
name, with pure hearts and clean hands, and look not forward any
more for another Messiah, then, at that time, the day will come
that it must needs be expedient that they should believe these things.*
2 NEPHI 25:16

God commanded "that [we] should love and serve
him, the only living and true God, and that he should
be the only being whom [we] should worship" (D&C
20:19). In our day the living Christ has instructed his
Saints to "fall down and worship the Father in my
name" (D&C 18:40). The perfect pattern is for us to
worship the Father, in the name of the Son, by the
power of the Holy Ghost. God the Father is the ultimate object of our worship; Jesus worshipped the
Father, and so must we. We worship Jesus Christ (2
Nephi 25:29) in the sense that we feel reverentially
grateful for his infinite and eternal atoning sacrifice
and for the perfect pattern of obedience he demonstrated. Because one of the highest forms of worship
is emulation, we worship the Son by striving to live as
he lived (3 Nephi 27:27). Christ is truly the prototype
of all saved beings (*Lectures on Faith*, 7:16).

Believe in Christ, and . . . be reconciled to God; for we know
that it is by grace that we are saved, after all we can do.
2 NEPHI 25:23

The grace of Jesus Christ makes salvation possible.
Each one of us needs this divine help in consequence
of the fall of Adam and our own weaknesses and mistakes. The grace of our Lord, manifest by his intimate
and infinite atoning sacrifice, is the means through
which we will be resurrected to immortality. His grace
grants us the capacity to repent and change (Mosiah
25–26), so that all humankind may "lay hold on eternal life and exaltation after they have expended their
own best efforts. . . . grace cannot suffice without total
effort on the part of the recipient" (Bible Dictionary,
s.v. "Grace"). We become new creatures in him by
doing all we can to live righteously (Mosiah
27:25–26). We exercise faith in him; we humbly
repent; we love and serve and remain steadfast to the
end. Without the grace of Christ, we falter and fail.
With his grace, we are able to "live, and move, and
have our being" (Acts 17:28).

*We talk of Christ, we rejoice in Christ, we preach of Christ,
we prophesy of Christ, and we write according to our prophecies,
that our children may know to what source they may
look for a remission of their sins.*

2 NEPHI 25:26

We are but one generation removed from apostasy. All we need to do to slide back into the Dark Ages is to refrain from teaching the gospel to the rising generation. All that is necessary for us to raise up a group of Latter-day Saints who are fully humanistic in character—who trust in their own genius and accomplishments—is to fail to teach Jesus Christ and him crucified. The Prophet Joseph Smith explained that the atonement of Christ is the fundamental principle of our religion and all other things that pertain to our religion are only appendages to it (*Teachings,* 121). Thus Nephi declared the doctrine of doctrines, the message of messages when he set forth the eternal truth that we talk, rejoice, preach, and prophesy of Christ so that our children and their children may know whence cometh their salvation and from whence happiness here and eternal reward hereafter are to come.

*Behold, my beloved brethren, I say unto you that the
Lord God worketh not in darkness.*

2 NEPHI 26:23

Since the early days of the Restoration individuals
and groups have claimed some new revelation, some
special insight not readily available to the Church as a
whole. That is, they pretend to some secret knowledge,
something untaught by those charged to teach the
Saints. The wisest among the people of the household
of faith learn to look regularly and hearken consistently
to the counsel and direction of the Lord's living oracles.
We have been instructed to teach "none other things
than that which the prophets and apostles have written" (D&C 52:9). "All they who receive the oracles of
God [the revelations of God, as given through his living
oracles] let them beware how they hold them lest they
are accounted as a light thing, and are brought under
condemnation thereby, and stumble and fall when the
storms descend, and the winds blow, and the rains
descend, and beat upon their house" (D&C 90:5). God
works with his people above board, in the light of day.

*He commandeth that there shall be no priestcrafts; for, behold,
priestcrafts are that men preach and set themselves up for a light
unto the world, that they might get gain and praise of the world;
but they seek not the welfare of Zion.*

2 NEPHI 26:29

Those who practice priestcraft are motivated by mammon, having "corrupt minds" (D&C 33:4). They might serve in Church positions or perform acts of charity in an effort to look good or cultivate contacts to enhance income, prominence, or career prospects. Nephi knew ours would be a day when priestcraft abounded (1 Nephi 22:23). He knew how insidious and spiritually deadly it can be and told us to beware. We would all do well to reflect: *What are my motivations and intentions? Do I seek the praise, honor, and money of the world more than the welfare of Zion? Do I seek to glorify God—or myself?* Pride is at the heart of priestcraft. Humility is the antidote. The Lord Jesus Christ is the Light of the world, and we are mere reflections—but only when our hearts are pure and our will is swallowed up in the will of the Master (Mosiah 15:7).

*The Lord God hath given a commandment that all men should
have charity, which charity is love. And except they
should have charity they were nothing.*
2 NEPHI 26:30

Charity, the essence of the gospel of Jesus Christ, is the Savior's pure love, the highest, noblest kind of love. We "pray unto the Father with all the energy of heart" to possess it (Moroni 7:48). To have our hearts filled with charity is the aspiration of all who seek to follow Jesus. Over time, almost imperceptibly, as we forget ourselves and reach out to others in love and kindness, we are blessed with charity. Those who serve with charity do so with a pure heart, having no desire but to build up the kingdom of God and establish his righteousness. The charitable person is without envy, pride, or concern for personal gain, prominence, and honor (Moroni 7:45, 47). Those who little by little, day by day, consecrate their lives to the cause of Christ manifest their commitment by small and simple acts of pure love. Charity is the anthem of Zion, the theme song of those striving to be true Saints.

MAY

Marvel not that all mankind . . .
must be born again; . . . and thus
they become new creatures;
and unless they do this, they
can in nowise inherit the
kingdom of God.
MOSIAH 27:25–26

The laborer in Zion shall labor for Zion;
for if they labor for money they shall perish.
2 NEPHI 26:31

If we labor for that which has eternal value, we will receive eternal rewards. But if we work to procure the fleeting prizes of this world, we will not have lasting rewards. When we die, as we all will, we can take nothing with us—at least, nothing of transitory worth. And yet, why do we spend so much time proudly pursuing such possessions, prestige, and power? The Lord told us, "If ye seek the riches which it is the will of the Father to give unto you, ye shall be the richest of all people, for ye shall have the riches of eternity; and it must needs be that the riches of the earth are mine to give; but beware of pride, lest ye become as the Nephites of old" (D&C 38:39). As we humbly center our efforts on that which has eternal value—the condition of our hearts and minds, our memories, and our loving relationships—we build Zion, one family at a time.

*He doeth nothing save it be plain unto the children of men; . . .
and he denieth none that come unto him, black and white,
bond and free, male and female; and he remembereth the heathen;
and all are alike unto God, both Jew and Gentile.*

2 NEPHI 26:33

In the days of Jesus, the gospel was delivered first to the Jews and later, through the ministries of the apostles Peter and Paul, to the Gentile nations (Matthew 10:5; 15:24; Acts 10). From the late 1830s there was in the restored church a restriction placed on who could bear the holy priesthood. In June 1978 this all was changed through revelation to a modern prophet. God loves all of his children and is no respecter of person (Acts 10:34; Romans 2:11; Colossians 3:25). There is, however, a divine timetable by which he acts, a sacred system by which things are brought to pass according to his omniscience. God "hath made of one blood all nations of men for to dwell on all the face of the earth, and hath determined the times before appointed" (Acts 17:26). Thus, the faithful move forward with perfect confidence in the Lord and his chosen servants, doing so "in all patience and faith" (D&C 21:5).

There shall also be many which shall say: Eat, drink, and be merry;
nevertheless, fear God—he will justify in committing a little sin; . . .
and if it so be that we are guilty, God will beat us with a few stripes,
and at last we shall be saved in the kingdom of God.

2 NEPHI 28:8

The great lie of our time is that life is a series of entertainments to be enjoyed without restraint or circumspection. We're often encouraged by such lies as *What's the harm if we sin a little? Who's to say what sin is? And what does it matter, if we all die anyway? If there really is a God, we'll be punished a little and then sent on our way to everlasting happiness.* Such is the thinking of the world because of the propaganda of the adversary and the beliefs of such antichrists as Sherem, Nehor, Korihor and modern-day charlatans preaching self-indulgence. God is indeed merciful and gracious. He is slow to anger and eager to accept the repentant sinner. But he is also faithful in the punishment of the evildoer, especially when the sinner has light and knowledge, for God "cannot look upon sin with the least degree of allowance" (D&C 1:31). We are to shun sin and steadfastly hold onto the iron rod.

They wear stiff necks and high heads; yea, and because of pride, and wickedness, and abominations, and whoredoms, they have all gone astray save it be a few, who are the humble followers of Christ; nevertheless, they are led, that in many instances they do err because they are taught by the precepts of men.

2 NEPHI 28:14

Hugh Nibley observed that "the words of the prophets cannot be held to the tentative and defective tests that men have devised for them. Science, philosophy, and common sense all have a right to their day in court. But the last word does not lie with them. . . . The last word is a testimony of the gospel that comes only by direct revelation. Our Father in heaven speaks it, and if it were in perfect agreement with the science of today, it would surely be out of line with the science of tomorrow. Let us not, therefore, seek to hold God to the learned opinions of the moment when he speaks the language of eternity" (*World and the Prophets*, 134). The humble followers of Christ must exercise discernment when they engage the philosophies of the world and the precepts of men. Human theories may serve a purpose to some extent, but we certainly would not want to build a foundation of faith on such shifting sand.

*Thus the devil cheateth their souls,
and leadeth them away carefully down to hell.*
2 NEPHI 28:21

Television, movies, the Internet, and other influences mock sacred things and entice with their beguiling wares. The sanctity of the home is under threat and so are our children, who need to grow and develop in an environment that allows them to become sensitive to the Spirit. Prophets have warned us for generations. President Spencer W. Kimball said: "We need to constantly guard against immorality, pornography, and sexual permissiveness that would destroy the purity of the family members. . . . We must be constantly alert to their evil presence in our homes and destroy them as we would the germs and filth of disease. We must hunt them from the closets of our minds, freeing ourselves of such worldliness, quenching the embers of wickedness before they become destructive flames" (*Ensign,* May 1979, 5–6). By zealously guarding our hearts and homes, we allow Christ and his gospel to take root and flourish in our souls.

Others will he pacify, and lull them away into carnal
security. . . . others he flattereth away, and . . . saith unto
them: I am no devil, for there is none. . . . Therefore,
wo be unto him that is at ease in Zion!

2 NEPHI 28:21–22, 24

The evil one is a master of deception. Sometimes he puts on sheep's clothing and with feigned gentleness leads many away. Other times, he is persuasive, cunning, and openly rebellious. His versatility makes him dangerous as he adapts his attack to our weaknesses. His sophistries sedate our spirit and keep us from recognizing our need for repentance. He would have us believe that we have nothing to worry about, for he does not exist or couldn't possibly hurt us. He tries to distract us with worldly cares and trap us in vice, carnality, and laziness, thereby causing us to lose feelings of divine discontent that lead us to forsake sin and call upon the Savior's atoning sacrifice. If we are not constantly on guard against evil, if we are not courageous in the fight against spiritual apathy, we risk being seized with "death, and hell, and the devil" (2 Nephi 28:23). Those who have enlisted in the Lord's army must ever be vigilant.

*Yea, wo be unto him that saith: We have received, and we need
no more! Wo be unto him that shall say: We have received
the word of God, and we need no more of the word
of God, for we have enough!*

2 NEPHI 28:27, 29

Nephi delivered many prophetic warnings concerning evil attitudes that would exist among the children of God in the last days. As if to save the worst attitude for last, Nephi focused at length upon man's sense of self-sufficiency, his complacency regarding receiving more of eternal truth. The Prophet Joseph Smith taught, "It is the constitutional disposition of mankind to set up stakes and set bounds to the works and ways of the Almighty" (*Teachings*, 320). One who is living beneath his or her spiritual privileges is put off and even offended when additional light and truth are offered, while that man or woman who delights in the truths of salvation and who seeks for deeper understanding is eager and excited to gain clarification, enlargement of soul, and an elevated perspective. It is to the latter that the "greater portion of the word," the mysteries of God, will come (Alma 12:10).

Know ye not that . . . I bring forth my word unto the children of men, yea, even upon all the nations of the earth? . . . Know ye not that the testimony of two nations is a witness unto you that I am God, that I remember one nation like unto another?

2 NEPHI 29:7–8

The Holy Bible is indeed the word of God. To this point in time, it has led more people of the earth to understand and accept the divinity of Jesus Christ and to abide by the basic laws of goodness and decency than any other book. We love the Bible. We cherish its teachings. But we do not believe its message is sufficient to direct the affairs of God's kingdom through all ages of time. What the Almighty counseled Enoch to do was insufficient to direct father Abraham. What Moses delivered to ancient Israel was insufficient to lead the early Christian church. To supplement the Bible is not to discredit it nor to contradict it. A living church requires a living tree of life—continuing revelation and additional scripture through living apostles and prophets. In the Lord's Church and kingdom, the canon of scripture will never be closed.

If ye shall follow the Son, with full purpose of heart, . . .
repenting of your sins, witnessing unto the Father that ye
are willing to take upon you the name of Christ, by baptism—
. . . behold, then shall ye receive the Holy Ghost.
2 NEPHI 31:13

The doctrine of Christ teaches that Jesus was baptized to fulfill all righteousness and to show us an example of humbly following the Father. Thus could he say, "Follow me, and do the things which ye have seen me do" (2 Nephi 31:13). Joseph Smith taught, "Baptism is a sign to God, to angels, and to heaven that we do the will of God, and there is no other way beneath the heavens whereby God hath ordained for man to come to Him to be saved, and enter into the Kingdom of God, except faith in Jesus Christ, repentance, and baptism for the remission of sins, and any other course is in vain; then you have the promise of the gift of the Holy Ghost" (*Teachings,* 198). We must enter the gate of baptism with full purpose of heart. As we humbly follow Christ and take his name upon us, our hearts become pure, and we become "new creatures" in Christ (Mosiah 27:26).

Yea, the words of my Beloved are true and faithful. He that endureth to the end, the same shall be saved. . . . unless a man shall endure to the end, in following the example of the Son of the living God, he cannot be saved.
2 NEPHI 31:15–16

All gospel truths, when properly understood, bring with them assurance and faith. They may be relied upon implicitly, for such truths lift and ameliorate. They never oppress and enslave. Those in possession of these eternal verities find that their confidence waxes strong in the presence of the Lord. Temporal truths, with all their value, bring no such assurance. A "fifth principle of the gospel" is enduring to the end, which consists in remaining faithful after baptism and keeping the commandments over the course of our lives (Alma 7:16). Salvation is the journey of a lifetime, not an event of some particular moment. By following the example of the Son of God, we have the perfect model and inspiration to remain steadfast and immovable to the end.

After ye have gotten into this strait and narrow path, I would ask
if all is done? Behold, I say unto you, Nay; for ye have not come
thus far save it were by the word of Christ with unshaken faith in
him, relying wholly upon the merits of him who is mighty to save.

2 NEPHI 31:19

To have faith in Christ is to rely upon him—to rely upon his goodness, his mercy, his merits, and his grace—to see us through the challenges and demands of this life and on into the next. Though the Master expects us to manifest our faithfulness through the performance of good works, our trust and our reliance must never be in ourselves or in our unaided efforts. True self-confidence comes only through our complete confidence in Christ, the One who is mighty to save. If our reliance is upon our own merits, then we will forevermore fall short of the ideal and will live and die frustrated and exhausted. We need to pray as if everything depended upon the Lord and then work as if everything depended upon . . . the Lord!

Wherefore, ye must press forward with a steadfastness in Christ, having a perfect brightness of hope, and a love of God and of all men. Wherefore, if ye shall press forward, feasting upon the word of Christ, and endure to the end, behold, thus saith the Father: Ye shall have eternal life.

2 NEPHI 31:20

Those who are steadfast in Christ pursue a course of obedience and righteousness. They go forward with a hope in Christ that liberates them from the darkness of doubt and despair. They come hungry to the Lord's banquet, feasting upon his doctrines, principles, and truths. They endure to the end and receive eternal life in the kingdom of God (Matthew 10:41). The Lord seals an exaltation upon them because of their faithfulness. The Lord gave that assurance to Alma in these words, "Thou art my servant; and I covenant with thee that thou shalt have eternal life; and thou shalt serve me and go forth in my name, and shall gather together my sheep" (Mosiah 26:20). And to the Prophet Joseph the Lord said, "I seal upon you your exaltation, and prepare a throne for you in the kingdom of my Father" (D&C 132:49). God's greatest gift to the faithful is the quality of life that he himself enjoys—eternal life.

How could ye speak with the tongue of angels save it were by the
Holy Ghost? Angels speak by the power of the Holy Ghost;
wherefore, they speak the words of Christ. Wherefore, . . .
feast upon the words of Christ; for behold, the words of
Christ will tell you all things what ye should do.

2 NEPHI 32:2–3

A man and his son attended the priesthood session
of general conference on a Saturday evening. The
meeting was a spiritual feast, particularly the closing
remarks given by the president of the Church. As the
large group exited the stake center, an older high priest
commented to his friend: "The prophet just spoke
with the tongue of angels." His friend nodded in the
affirmative. The son turned to his father and asked,
"What did he mean, Dad?" The father answered that
the living prophet had spoken by the power of the
Holy Ghost and thus had spoken the words of
Christ—he had said what Christ would have said if He
had given the closing address. He explained that to
"speak with the tongue of angels" was to speak by the
Spirit, to deliver a message that would be in harmony
with what angels would deliver, for "angels speak by
the power of the Holy Ghost; wherefore, they speak
the words of Christ."

MAY 14

I, Nephi, cannot write all the things which were taught among my people; neither am I mighty in writing, like unto speaking; for when a man speaketh by the power of the Holy Ghost the power of the Holy Ghost carrieth it unto the hearts of the children of men.

2 NEPHI 33:1

A modern revelation affirms that "the Spirit shall be given unto you by the prayer of faith; and if ye receive not the Spirit ye shall not teach" (D&C 42:14). This declaration is both a command and a prophecy. In one sense, we should not even attempt to convey sacred things by any power other than the power of the Spirit (1 Corinthians 2:11–14). If we do try to teach "by some other way"—such as by the power of the intellect alone—it is not of God (D&C 50:18), and thus true spiritual communication will not take place. On the other hand, when a gospel teacher prepares well, organizes the material, and then seeks and receives the empowering and enlightening influence of the Holy Ghost, the message is carried to the hearts of those who listen. That is the foundation for true conversion.

[Nephi] gave me, Jacob, a commandment that I should write upon these plates a few of the things which I considered to be most precious; that I should not touch, save it were lightly, concerning the history of this people which are called the people of Nephi.

JACOB 1:2

Although Lehi, Nephi, Jacob, Alma, Abinadi, Moroni, Jared, and Ether were real people who lived in a real place at a real point in earth's history, the Book of Mormon is predominantly a collection of sacred teachings concerning the doctrine of Christ. To be sure, those teachings are placed in a historical context, but the most important aspect of the Nephite-Jaredite record is its sacred witness of the Lord and Savior Jesus Christ. Jacob was instructed that the small plates of Nephi were to consist largely of sacred preaching, great revelation, and prophecy, but even the large plates of Nephi, known generally as a more secular account (dealing with wars, journeyings, and kingships) place the prophetic word and the doctrinal proclamations alongside historical events. In a very real way, the Book of Mormon is not just a history book. Rather, it is the saga of a message, a testament of Christ.

We labored diligently among our people, that we might persuade
them to come unto Christ, and partake of the goodness of God,
that they might enter into his rest.

JACOB 1:7

The purpose of the Book of Mormon and the restored gospel is to persuade all people to come unto Christ. All else that we do is ancillary to this testimony and message. But coming unto Christ is much more than an intellectual confession of our need for a Savior. It is knowing, by the witness of the Spirit, that he is God's Almighty Son and that salvation is found only in and through his holy name. As we come unto Christ, we gain the quiet, powerful assurance that the Lord reigns, that the gospel has been restored, that God has empowered his oracles in this day to represent him. And we act accordingly. Such faithful obedience invites the peace of God into our lives and helps us to meet the challenges of mortality—and eventually to inherit the fulness of the Father's glory (Moroni 7:3; D&C 84:24). The goodness of God and the blessing of eternal life are heaven's most glorious gifts.

It grieveth me that I must use so much boldness of speech
concerning you, before your wives and your children, many of
whose feelings are exceedingly tender and chaste and delicate
before God, which thing is pleasing unto God.

JACOB 2:7

Anyone who has had responsibility within the church and kingdom of God knows how difficult it is to address such sensitive issues as chastity and virtue. Within the class or congregation, there are inevitably two kinds of people: those who have maintained their virtue and those who have not. The speaker or teacher is challenged to warn the former to avoid at all costs this particular sin, while at the same time holding out to the latter the message of hope and possible forgiveness. It would be wonderful if the leaders of the Church could spend most of their time preaching "the pleasing word of God, yea, the word which healeth the wounded soul" (Jacob 2:8), but unfortunately there are those who need to be summoned to repent and to face up to their sinful actions. Thus, those charged to lead must occasionally use boldness of speech, yearning all the while for the Spirit of God to provide personal tutorials for those who listen.

Think of your brethren like unto yourselves,
and be familiar with all and free with your substance,
that they may be rich like unto you.

JACOB 2:17

By possessing charity, the pure love of Christ, and sharing our abundance with the less fortunate, we free ourselves and others from the shackles of sin (D&C 49:20; 104:17–18). To achieve Zion, we must have a free and open union upheld by God's laws. People of varying social, economic, and spiritual backgrounds can all have place in God's kingdom if they do what is required. Zion is a people who are "of one heart and one mind," a people who dwell "in righteousness; and there [is] no poor among them" (Moses 7:18). The word *familiar* is from the same root as the word *family:* to be familiar with all is to treat all others as members of the family, to extend the fellowship and love and resources of the family to all who stand in need. In other words, it is to establish Zion, or heaven on earth. Such association here is but a preparation for that which is to come hereafter.

*Before ye seek for riches, seek ye for the kingdom of God. And
after ye have obtained a hope in Christ ye shall obtain riches,
if ye seek them; and ye will seek them for the intent to do good—
to . . . administer relief to the sick and the afflicted.*
JACOB 2:18–19

Jacob soberly denounced the love of riches and the
pride it engenders. If we seek for riches, we must
desire to use our prosperity to lift and bless others.
Even so, not all who hope in Christ and have the pure
intent to help their fellowmen will have material prosperity. Faithful followers of Christ must not succumb
to the temptation to equate financial success with personal righteousness. Too many righteous persons who
have known *true* success in life have lived and died in
humble circumstances for us to suppose that being
good could be equated with being affluent. But this we
know: where one's treasure is, there will his heart be
also (Matthew 6:21). Riches can be a blessing or a burden—it all depends on how we regard them and what
we do with them. If our focus is on the things of eternity and that which matters most, we can use our
abundance to bless God's children and build his
kingdom.

They understand not the scriptures, for they seek to excuse them-
selves in committing whoredoms. . . . Behold, David and Solomon
truly had many wives and concubines, which thing was
abominable before me, saith the Lord. For if I will, saith the Lord
of Hosts, raise up seed unto me, I will command my people.

JACOB 2:23–24, 30

Jacob was concerned about unauthorized plural marriages, unions that did not have divine sanction. In
ancient Israel a concubine was a legal wife with a lower
social standing but a wife nonetheless. In the Book of
Mormon, however, the word *concubine* tends to be used
much as we would use the words *mistress* or *paramour.*
There were times in antiquity when God commanded
his people to enter into plural marriages, but both David
and Solomon were guilty of entering into such relationships illicitly and without divine consent (2 Samuel 11,
12; 1 Kings 11). With immorality widespread in Judea at
the time the Lehites left Jerusalem for America
(Jeremiah 5:7–8), Jehovah specifically commanded
Father Lehi that plural marriages not be contracted by
his descendants (Jacob 2:34; 3:5). In short, monogamy is
the rule and polygamy is the exception, an exception that
can be made only by God through his anointed servants
(Jacob 2:30; D&C 132:38–39; Smith, *Teachings,* 324).

Ye have broken the hearts of your tender wives, and lost the confidence of your children, because of your bad examples before them; and the sobbings of their hearts ascend up to God against you.

JACOB 2:35

Enduring love and trust are the foundation of a happy marriage and celestial family. The gift of procreation is from God, the Father of our spirits; this sacred power, when channeled and expressed appropriately within the bonds of matrimony, ennobles and sanctifies the marital union. But nothing shatters hope and destroys familial feelings as profoundly as sexual infidelity. Who can calculate the wounds of immorality that echo down the generations? The ravages of wanton sin bring the desecration of the soul. Pain, guilt, mourning, sorrow, and shattered dreams follow in the wake of selfish misuse of sacred powers. Such sins will be sorely punished by a just God, whose heart is tender toward his offended ones. Our actions and examples are either for or against the next generation. Long after our words and teachings are forgotten, our posterity will reflect upon our lives and hearken to our example (Jacob 3:10).

A hundredth part of the proceedings of this people,
which now began to be numerous,
cannot be written upon these plates.

JACOB 3:13

Knowing that only a small part of the history and teachings of the Nephites is found in the Book of Mormon (Words of Mormon 1:5; 3 Nephi 5:8; 26:6; Ether 15:33), knowing that Nephi and Mormon and Moroni saw our day and clearly understood the nature of our challenges (Mormon 8:35; 9:30), and knowing that these prophet-editors were inspired in their selection of teachings that would do the most to settle doctrinal disputes and lead men and women to Christ—knowing all these things, we ought to read the Book of Mormon with reverence and awe, for we have been given that which is appropriate and needful for our time. This sacred book was written for us; its message is both timely and timeless, and we will be blessed abundantly as we feast upon its words.

*For this intent have we written these things, that they may know
that we knew of Christ, and we had a hope of his glory many
hundred years before his coming; and not only we
ourselves had a hope of his glory, but also all the
holy prophets which were before us.*

JACOB 4:4

The apostle Peter taught concerning the Messiah
that "to him give all the prophets witness, that through
his name whosoever believeth in him shall receive
remission of sins" (Acts 10:43). The principal role of
a prophet is to stand as a special witness of Christ,
inasmuch as the testimony of Jesus is the spirit of
prophecy (Revelation 19:10). Latter-day Saints declare
that prophets from the beginning of time have fore-
seen and foreknown the coming of the Lord Jesus
Christ, have understood his gospel or plan of salvation,
and have officiated in its saving ordinances. Thus,
from the beginning, those who have looked to his
coming have enjoyed "a hope of his glory," that
through him happiness here and eternal reward hereafter are available to the penitent.

We search the prophets, and we have many revelations and the spirit of prophecy; and having all these witnesses we obtain a hope, and our faith becometh unshaken, insomuch that we truly can command in the name of Jesus and the very trees obey us, or the mountains, or the waves of the sea.

JACOB 4:6

The more experience we have with the Spirit of the Lord, the more we are able to engage the challenges of life, including the false doctrines and spurious educational ideas that often strike at the foundation of our faith. Those who have entered the realm of divine experience—who have sought the gifts of the Spirit, have received the gift of the Holy Ghost, and have taken that gift as a guide in life—come to acquire a hope in Christ, the expectation, anticipation, and assurance that in and through the Holy Messiah they will be saved. Their trust and confidence in the Lord, his plan, and his Church thereby become unshakable.

Behold, great and marvelous are the works of the Lord. How unsearchable are the depths of the mysteries of him; and it is impossible that man should find out all his ways. And no man knoweth of his ways save it be revealed unto him.

JACOB 4:8

In his great Intercessory Prayer, the Savior stated that it is life eternal to know God and Jesus Christ whom he has sent (John 17:3). We come to know them through learning of their constancy, their goodness and mercy, and their unwavering love for all humankind. As we cultivate the gift of the Holy Ghost and thereby gain "the mind of Christ" (1 Corinthians 2:16), our service to others (and thus to them) becomes consistent and steadfast (Mosiah 5:13, 15). As we experience the love of God in our own lives, we are thereby empowered to love others by becoming instruments of divine peace. We shall never in this life understand fully the marvelous and mysterious workings of the Almighty. But one day we will know as we are known, such that "when he shall appear, we shall be like him, for we shall see him as he is" (Moroni 7:48; 1 John 3:2; D&C 76:94).

Seek not to counsel the Lord, but to take counsel from his hand. For behold, ye yourselves know that he counseleth in wisdom, and in justice, and in great mercy, over all his works.

JACOB 4:10

Sometimes we may feel like complaining to the Lord about a challenge or difficulty that has come to us, often through no fault of our own. "God knows what is best for us," counseled Elder Richard G. Scott. "Although we may not understand why we experience some things now, in His timetable we will know and be grateful. He has promised to help us with our burdens" (*Ensign,* November 1999, 88). An eternal perspective will help us to "be still" and know that all things will work together for our good if we are humble and teachable. The Lord instructs and refines us, sometimes in the furnace of affliction, so that we can develop the attributes of godliness. He who is perfect in wisdom, justice, and mercy knows us individually and wants for us a fulness of joy. His promise is sure: "Peace I leave with you, my peace I give unto you: not as the world giveth, give I unto you. Let not your heart be troubled, neither let it be afraid" (John 14:27).

*The Jews were a stiffnecked people; and they despised the words of
plainness, and killed the prophets, and sought for things that they
could not understand. Wherefore, because of their blindness,
which blindness came by looking beyond the mark,
they must needs fall.*

JACOB 4:14

It has frequently been observed that the gospel of
Jesus Christ is simply beautiful and beautifully simple.
Yet the gospel is far-reaching, broad as eternity, deep
and penetrating. Surely the more we pursue a serious
study of the principles and doctrines of the
Restoration, the more we recognize the complexities
of the Lord's divine plan. Prayerful and wise continuation in that study, however, should lead us to a simplicity beyond complexity. Simply stated, it just may
be that the more we learn, the less we teach, for we
begin to sense the need to focus primarily upon saving doctrines and principles. Those who have been
born of the Spirit are seldom guilty of looking beyond
the mark, especially when the mark is Christ. Rather,
they teach the gospel with simplicity and in a way that
encourages the confirming and enlightening influence
of the Holy Spirit.

*By the stumbling of the Jews they will reject the stone upon which
they might build and have safe foundation. But behold . . . this
stone shall become the great, and the last, and the only sure
foundation, upon which the Jews can build.*

JACOB 4:15–16

Jacob was well aware that the Jews will stumble by
rejecting their true Messiah, his gospel, and his church.
And yet he was also aware that Christ will one day
serve as their only sure foundation. How is this possible? The answer remains a mystery to those of the
world, for it concerns the works and ways of an infinite being and the manner in which the Almighty will
bring to pass his purposes through his covenant
people. That mystery is set forth in the allegory of
Zenos, one of the most magnificent but least understood passages of scripture concerning the destiny of
the house of Israel (Jacob 5–6).

Behold, thus saith the Lord, I will liken thee, O house of Israel, like unto a tame olive-tree, which a man took and nourished in his vineyard; and it grew, and waxed old, and began to decay.

JACOB 5:3

The allegory of Zenos is filled with symbols: olive trees, graftings, roots, branches, vineyards. It is a statement of how God, through his covenant people, blesses the entire world. We need not understand the meaning of every symbol in this allegory in order to grasp its central message: God simply will not let Israel go! His patience and long-suffering are truly infinite with the people who have been "most precious unto him from the beginning" (Jacob 5:74). "And how merciful is our God unto us, for he remembereth the house of Israel, both roots and branches; and he stretches forth his hands unto them all the day long." The call is for the chosen people to "cleave unto God as he cleaveth unto you" (Jacob 6:4–5).

He had a perfect knowledge of the language of the people;
wherefore, he could use much flattery, and much power of speech,
according to the power of the devil.

JACOB 7:4

Like any antichrist, Sherem lived in denial: he
denied the things of God, including the coming of
Christ, as well as the spirit of prophecy and revelation.
He knew what he knew, and the parameters of that
knowledge were restricted. He knew the natural
world, the things that we perceive through our five
senses. Further, he suffered from a means-end sickness, for he confused the type with that toward which
it pointed. He languished in a massive overgeneraliza-
tion—because he did not know, no one else knew,
either. His demand for a sign or tangible evidence was
but a manifestation of the emptiness of his soul, for he
reveled in that which he knew best: the physical and
the fanciful. True faith does not come by signs, but
signs follow those who believe. As is often the case,
sign-seeking brings not confirmation but divine wrath
and condemnation (D&C 63:9, 11), and so it was with
Sherem.

*I will tell you of the wrestle which I had before God,
before I received a remission of my sins.*

ENOS 1:2

Not all prayers are alike. Often the depth and intensity of our prayers are related directly to the most pressing needs in our life at the time. Enos had surely witnessed the power of God as it rested upon his father. But there came a time in Enos's life, just as there will surely come in our own, when he wanted to know for sure, when he desired to be right with God. Enos remembered what his father had said concerning eternal life and the joy of the Saints, and, perhaps for the first time in his life, such other-worldly concepts became real and desirable. After Enos continued in prayer for many hours, God opened the heavens, spoke peace to him, and gave wholeness to his soul. His faith and trust in the Holy One of Israel opened the door to unspeakable joy and unshakable conviction.

June

Have ye spiritually been born of God? Have ye received his image in your countenances? Have ye experienced this mighty change in your hearts?

Alma 5:14

I rejoice in the day when my mortal shall put on immortality, and shall stand before him; then shall I see his face with pleasure, and he will say unto me: Come unto me, ye blessed, there is a place prepared for you in the mansions of my Father. Amen.

ENOS 1:27

The scriptures teach that we should work out our salvation with fear and trembling before the Lord (Philippians 2:12). The word translated here as *fear* implies to reverence or respect, not to cower beneath the wrath of a vengeful being. As members of the Church of Jesus Christ live so as to cultivate the influence of the Holy Ghost, they grow in confidence before God (1 John 2:28; D&C 121:45). That is, they come to know that the course in life they are pursuing is according to the will of God and that they, although not yet perfect in this life, will enjoy peace in this world as a harbinger to eternal life in the world to come.

The prophets, and the priests, and the teachers, did labor diligently, exhorting with all long-suffering the people to diligence; teaching the law of Moses, and the intent for which it was given; persuading them to look forward unto the Messiah, and believe in him to come as though he already was.

JAROM 1:11

For the faithful among the Nephites, it was as though prophecy had become history. They looked to Christ and his atonement for salvation and lived the principles and ordinances of his gospel as though his ministry and atoning sacrifice had already come to pass. Theirs was a pure faith, a reliance born of the Spirit of God. They understood clearly that the great act of reconciliation was retroactive and that Jesus was indeed the Lamb slain from the foundation of the world (Revelation 13:8; Moses 7:47). They were "made alive in Christ because of [their] faith" (2 Nephi 25:25). Thus, it was "shown unto the people, a great many thousand years before his coming, that even redemption should come unto them" (Helaman 8:18; compare Alma 39:17–19).

Yea, come unto him, and offer your whole souls as an offering unto him, and continue in fasting and praying, and endure to the end; and as the Lord liveth ye will be saved.

OMNI 1:26

The apostle Paul encouraged the Saints at Rome to "present your bodies a living sacrifice, holy, acceptable unto God, which is your reasonable service" (Romans 12:1). Though it is a noble deed to die for the faith, it is even more commendable to give one's life in faithful service to the kingdom of God. As disciples of Christ, we are called upon to sacrifice our time, our talents, and our resources to the establishment of Zion. Perhaps more importantly, we are called upon to sacrifice ourselves, to put to death the old man of sin—to nail it to the cross of Christ, as it were (Galatians 2:20)—and to come forth unto a newness of life, to become new creatures in Christ (2 Corinthians 5:17; Mosiah 27:26). The submission of our will and the surrender of our soul constitute the broken heart and contrite spirit so central to becoming a follower of the lowly Nazarene.

I do this for a wise purpose; for thus it whispereth me, according to the workings of the Spirit of the Lord which is in me. And now, I do not know all things; but the Lord knoweth all things which are to come; wherefore, he worketh in me to do according to his will.

WORDS OF MORMON 1:7

Words of Mormon serves as a transition between the small plates of Nephi and Mormon's abridgment of the large plates. At this point in his work, Mormon felt impressed to include the unabridged small plates within his larger collection of sacred writings, but he did not know why. The complete vision of the future, including the call of Joseph Smith, the delivery of the golden plates, and the eventual loss of the 116 pages of manuscript was not given to him at this time. What he did know was the Spirit of the Lord, and he knew to obey it and follow its direction. Our God does know all things, and for him the past, the present, and the future are and were "one eternal 'now'" (Smith, *Teachings,* 220). What the prophet-editor did was a part of the wise purpose of the Lord, for as Mormon declared, God "worketh in me to do according to his will."

I have not commanded you to come up hither to trifle with the words which I shall speak, but that you should hearken unto me, and open your ears that ye may hear, and your hearts that ye may understand, and your minds that the mysteries of God may be unfolded to your view.

MOSIAH 2:9

The Prophet Joseph Smith wrote: "Thy mind, O man! If thou wilt lead a soul unto salvation, must stretch as high as the utmost heavens, and search into and contemplate the darkest abyss, and the broad expanse of eternity—thou must commune with God. . . . None but fools will trifle with the souls of men" (*Teachings*, 137). King Benjamin felt the need to discourse upon the central truth of eternity—redemption and salvation in Christ. Thus he pleaded with his people not to trifle with his words but to listen and feel and think in such a way that the mysteries of God might be impressed upon their souls. Faith, or true conversion, comes through hearing the word of God (Romans 10:17), feeling the word of God (3 Nephi 19:32–33; D&C 8:2–3), and reflecting upon that word, so that the words of eternal life not only occupy our minds but press themselves upon our feelings (D&C 128:1).

If ye should serve him who has created you from the beginning,
and is preserving you from day to day, by lending you breath,
that ye may live and move and do according to your own
will . . . I say, if ye should serve him with all your whole
souls yet ye would be unprofitable servants.

MOSIAH 2:21

King Benjamin set forth in beautiful simplicity the doctrine of divine indebtedness, the supernal concept that all we are, all we possess, and all we can ever hope to become totally depends upon the transcendent mercy and goodness of God. A modern revelation counsels us to "thank the Lord thy God in all things" and teaches us that "in nothing doth man offend God, or against none is his wrath kindled, save those who confess not his hand in all things, and obey not his commandments" (D&C 59:7, 21). We are also told, "He that receiveth of God, let him account it of God; and let him rejoice that he is accounted of God worthy to receive" (D&C 50:34). Because we cannot, worlds without end, work ourselves into celestial glory, we will forever be "unprofitable servants," eternally indebted to the Gods of heaven for the very breath we breathe. Such recognition, such submission, such surrender is prerequisite to spiritual strength.

The time cometh, and is not far distant, that with power, the Lord
Omnipotent who reigneth, who was, and is from all eternity to
all eternity, shall come down from heaven among the children
of men, and shall dwell in a tabernacle of clay, and shall
go forth amongst men, working mighty miracles.

MOSIAH 3:5

King Benjamin set forth a series of powerful teachings made known to him by an angel of God. Central
to all that Benjamin conveyed is the doctrine of the
incarnation, the condescension of God (compare 1
Nephi 11:16). Benjamin explained that the Lord
Omnipotent, the great Jehovah, the God of Abraham,
Isaac, and Jacob, would choose to leave his divine
throne, set aside his glory for a season, and dwell
among the children of men. Because he would take a
physical body, he would come to know the pains and
sicknesses and temptations and frustrations and infirmities of the flesh, an experience necessary for him to
gain complete empathy with mere mortals (Alma
7:11–12). Jesus was thereby enabled to consecrate himself as a substitutionary offering for all humankind.
Jesus Christ becomes our advocate with the Father,
one who knows "the weakness of man and how to
succor them who are tempted" (D&C 62:1).

He shall suffer temptations, and pain of body, hunger,
thirst, and fatigue, even more than man can suffer,
except it be unto death; for behold, blood cometh from
every pore, so great shall be his anguish for the wickedness
and the abominations of his people.

MOSIAH 3:7

Christ suffered in Gethsemane and on Golgotha even more than man can suffer, for surely he was more than man. As the literal Son of God the Father, he possesses within himself the powers of immortality (John 10:17–18; Helaman 5:11). Because of his divine inheritance as well as his consummate righteousness, he was entitled to a fulness of the Father's Spirit (JST John 3:34), which fulness he enjoyed throughout his life. While in the Garden and again while on the cross, Jesus experienced something he had never known: what it felt like to lose the sacred, sustaining influence of the Father's Spirit. The loss of that Spirit—which came as he assumed our burdens and our sins, as he became "sin for us" (2 Corinthians 5:21)—caused him to "tremble because of pain, and to bleed at every pore, and to suffer both body and spirit" (D&C 19:18; see also Luke 22:44; Young, *Journal of Discourses,* 3:206).

*Even if it were possible that little children could sin they could
not be saved; but I say unto you they are blessed; for behold,
as in Adam, or by nature, they fall, even so the blood
of Christ atoneth for their sins.*

MOSIAH 3:16

Religionists for centuries have asked, "Are little
children innocent?" For Latter-day Saints this is a
needless question, for surely all children are innocent.
The real question, however, is "Why are they innocent?" Humanists might answer that little children are
innocent because they are simply that way by nature:
they are sensitive, caring, willing to share, patient, and
never prone to pout. Most of us who have had children of our own, however, would conclude otherwise.
Little children are innocent because they are decreed
innocent as one of the unconditional benefits of the
infinite atonement of Christ. Thus the invitation for
all of us to become as little children (Matthew 18:3;
Moroni 8:10) is not alone a call to be submissive,
meek, humble, patient, full of love, and willing to submit (Mosiah 3:19) but also to be declared innocent by
virtue of Christ's atonement.

I say unto you, that there shall be no other name given nor any other way nor means whereby salvation can come unto the children of men, only in and through the name of Christ, the Lord Omnipotent.

MOSIAH 3:17

King Benjamin is the only Book of Mormon writer to use *omnipotent* to describe the Lord (Mosiah 3:5, 17, 18, 21; 5:2, 15). How fitting that this great prophet-king acknowledges that it is Jesus Christ who has unlimited and universal power, authority, and force; Jesus, who is the "Potentate, the King of kings, and Lord of lords" (1 Timothy 6:15). How appropriate that the scriptures capitalize the word *king* only when referring to the King of all the earth (Psalm 47:7), the Lord Jesus Christ who is the central figure in our doctrine and religious practice. We do all that we do in the name of the Son. We are saved from sin and rescued from death because of our loving Savior. No other name will do, no other means will bring "peace in this world, and eternal life in the world to come" (D&C 59:23).

The natural man is an enemy to God, and has been from the fall of Adam, and will be, forever and ever, unless he yields to the enticings of the Holy Spirit, and putteth off the natural man and becometh a saint through the atonement of Christ the Lord.

MOSIAH 3:19

Because we are the offspring of God, we have a divine nature. But we are born into a world of wickedness, sin, and temptation. We become natural, or carnal, by rebelling against God, succumbing to the world's enticements, or being tainted by its attitudes. In all dispensations, the Lord's people have been called *Saints*, manifesting that they have separated themselves from worldliness and are seeking to become a holy people by obedience to the laws and ordinances of the gospel. The atonement of Jesus Christ is an act of love by which all of us may cease to be God's enemies and become sanctified (Moroni 10:32–33). Becoming a Saint is the labor of a lifetime, a process rather than a singular spiritual experience or event. The Lord has said, "Except ye be converted, and become as little children, ye shall not enter into the kingdom of heaven" (Matthew 18:3). Our unconditional surrender to God restores in us the innocence, the simplicity and faith and unwavering trust, of little children.

After they had spoken these words the Spirit of the Lord came upon them, and they were filled with joy, having received a remission of their sins, and having peace of conscience, because of the exceeding faith which they had in Jesus Christ who should come.

MOSIAH 4:3

Each of us has asked at one time or another, "When is my repentance complete? When is it okay to stop repenting of this sin? How will I know when I have been forgiven?" Mormon, who thus delivers to us one of the priceless treasures of the Book of Mormon, declared that we know a particular sin has been remitted when we feel joy, when we feel peace of conscience, when we no longer feel the need to browbeat ourselves, when what we once did now seems so very foreign to who we have become. Inasmuch as the Spirit of the Lord cannot dwell in an unclean tabernacle, what do we conclude when we have begun once again to feel the impressions and cleansing influence of that Spirit in our lives? Simply stated, we are no longer unclean. The sin is behind us, and we have begun to walk in newness of life. We bury the old man of sin and have no intention of revisiting the cemetery (Romans 6:4–6).

Ye will not suffer your children that they go hungry, or naked;
neither will ye suffer that they transgress the laws of God, and
fight and quarrel one with another, and serve the devil. . . . ye will
teach them to love one another, and to serve one another.

MOSIAH 4:14–15

Parents have a solemn responsibility to care, both temporally and spiritually, for their children. They are to feed and clothe their children, provide them with opportunities for growth and development, and protect them from harm. Worthy parents in Zion also nurture their children's souls in spirituality. "Parents have a sacred duty to rear their children in love and righteousness" (Proclamation on the Family). They are to guide their children in the gospel, teach them to love and serve others, bring them up in light and truth, and help them learn to resist temptation and to choose the Lord's way of peace in this life and eternal joy in the world to come. How we fulfill these serious responsibilities will in large measure determine our happiness both here and hereafter. It is the most important work that we do, an eternal stewardship from which we will never be released. All earthly callings come and go, all temporal assignments surely fade away, but parenthood lasts forever.

I would that ye should impart of your substance to the poor, every man according to that which he hath, such as feeding the hungry, clothing the naked, visiting the sick and administering to their relief, both spiritually and temporally, according to their wants.

MOSIAH 4:26

We are to do more than think about, or even pray for, those in need. We are to *do* for others. Ours is a gospel of work, of action, of serving and blessing others. "Reach out in love to those who need our strength," counseled President Gordon B. Hinckley. "There are many among us who lie alone in pain. Medicine helps, but kind words can bring to pass miracles. Many there are who walk in frightening circumstances, fearful and unable to cope. There are good bishops and Relief Society officers who are available to help, but these cannot do it all. Each of us can and must be anxiously engaged" (*Stand a Little Taller*, 67). Focusing on our own spiritual and temporal welfare to the exclusion of others is not enough if we wish to dwell with God and Christ. True disciples follow the Master's example and go about doing good.

If ye do not watch yourselves, and your thoughts, and your words,
and your deeds, and observe the commandments of God,
and continue in the faith . . . ye must perish. And now,
O man, remember, and perish not.

MOSIAH 4:30

Temptation and sin surround us daily. Good behavior gets no time off, no respite from the great effort to resist the adversary and overcome our weaknesses. Ours is the struggle of a lifetime. To the apostles in the New World, Christ said, "Ye must watch and pray always, lest ye be tempted by the devil, and ye be led away captive by him" (3 Nephi 18:15). We must be constantly on guard as we watch our thoughts (Do we have lustful, jealous, or hateful feelings?), our words (Do we profane, gossip, speak evil of others?), and our deeds (Do our actions reflect integrity of heart?). We all fall short and make mistakes, but as long as we're repenting, improving day by day, sincerely striving to keep the commandments, and putting off the natural man, the Lord will bless us, and we will enter into his rest.

*We believe all the words which thou hast spoken unto us . . .
because of the Spirit of the Lord Omnipotent, which has wrought
a mighty change in us, or in our hearts, that we have no more disposition to do evil, but to do good continually.*

MOSIAH 5:2

Those who truly desire righteousness with all their souls are of one heart and one mind. They are anxiously engaged and steadfast in their holy endeavors. They are united in new knowledge, new insights, and new directions to life. The mighty change, a quiet but powerful process, results in an educated conscience, educated desires, educated and bridled passions. One with a change of attitude and character will not continue in sin (JST 1 John 3:8). A sincere yearning to do good and abhor evil accompanies those who are received into the family of Jesus Christ (Mosiah 5:7; D&C 25:1). Old things are put away, and a new life begins. That does not mean the road will become easy or life will be free of pain or temptation. But unwavering commitment to Christ and his kingdom keeps our eye single to the path of righteousness. To become changed is but a beginning—the journey of faith lies ahead.

Because of the covenant which ye have made ye shall be called the children of Christ, his sons, and his daughters; . . . for ye say that your hearts are changed through faith on his name; therefore, ye are born of him and have become his sons and his daughters.

MOSIAH 5:7

Lehi taught us that because of the Fall, all men and women are in a lost and fallen state and will remain so unless they rely upon our Divine Redeemer (1 Nephi 10:6). Because of the Fall, we experience spiritual death and are thus alienated from God and things of righteousness. Further, we are alienated from the family of God and thereby become, in a sense, spiritual orphans. The atonement of Christ does more than forgive our sins and cleanse our souls; it reinstates us into the family of God, and we become the sons and daughters of Jesus Christ by adoption. He becomes the Father of our rebirth, the Father of our redemption, the Father of our resurrection, the Father of our salvation. Through the gospel covenant and through being born again, we take upon us the family name, the name of Christ, and we are expected to live in a way that will bring dignity and respectability to that holy name.

*A seer is a revelator and a prophet also; and a gift which is greater
can no man have, except he should possess the power of God. . . .
But a seer can know of things which are past, and also things
which are to come, and by them shall all things be revealed.*

MOSIAH 8:16–17

All seers are prophets, but not all prophets are seers.
A prophet is one who knows by the power of the Holy
Ghost that Jesus is the Christ (Revelation 19:10).
Moses said anciently, "Would God that all the Lord's
people were prophets, and that the Lord would put his
spirit upon them" (Numbers 11:29). We are partakers
of the spirit of prophecy when our souls receive a
burning witness that Jesus Christ is the Son of God,
our Savior and Redeemer. Seers are given a special
endowment to see with spiritual eyes the past, present,
and future; a seer is a visionary in the highest sense,
one who can "see afar off" (Moses 6:27). Today we
sustain the First Presidency and the Quorum of the
Twelve Apostles as prophets, seers, and revelators for
the whole Church. We know they are the Lord's
authorized servants because of the surety of their witness and because of the priesthood keys they possess.

When king Noah had heard of the words which Abinadi had spoken unto the people, he was also wroth; and he said: Who is Abinadi, that I and my people should be judged of him, or who is the Lord, that shall bring upon my people such great affliction?
MOSIAH 11:27

From the beginning, there have always been those who challenged the Lord's anointed with such questions as, "Who is the Lord?" or "Who are his servants?" Refusing to heed the words of a prophet, such naysayers fall prey to pride (Moses 5:16; Exodus 5:2; Alma 9:2–6). Trusting in their own thoughts and abilities, they insulate themselves against the truth. A sure test of the truth of a prophet's message is the anger it kindles in the hearts of the wicked. Life-changing truths always seem to draw fire—especially when, like Noah and his priests, at one time they knew better. But by repeatedly giving in to the natural man, they become strangers to the truth until, finally, too much is at stake—position, possessions, and power—to heed the words of a man preaching righteousness. Easier to ignore, denounce, and reject than to let a grain of condemning truth enter their hard hearts. May our hearts always remain softened and open to the teachings of prophets.

*Ye have perverted the ways of the Lord. Ye have not applied your
hearts to understanding; therefore, ye have not been wise.
Therefore, what teach ye this people?*

MOSIAH 12:26–27

The priests of Noah did not possess the greater wisdom that comes from the heart, for they had closed themselves off to the whisperings of the Spirit. They may have known gospel principles, but they were clearly not living them. Speaking of those of his day who rejected him, the Savior needed only to repeat what had been said of the people of Isaiah's day: "For this people's heart is waxed gross, and their ears are dull of hearing, and their eyes they have closed; lest at any time they should see with their eyes, and hear with their ears, and should understand with their heart, and should be converted, and I should heal them" (Matthew 13:15; Isaiah 6:9–10). What good does it do to have knowledge and no wisdom, learning but no understanding, information but no spiritual insight? To be wise is to be humble and teachable. To follow the Master is to live and teach the truths of the gospel (D&C 88:81).

I say unto you, that salvation doth not come by the law alone; and were it not for the atonement, which God himself shall make for the sins and iniquities of his people, that they must unavoidably perish, notwithstanding the law of Moses.
MOSIAH 13:28

Unless we live the laws of God perfectly, we cannot qualify for salvation through our own works (2 Nephi 2:5). Salvation did not come anciently through the works of the law of Moses, nor does it come to us in modern times through observance of the commandments of God. Salvation is the greatest of all the gifts of God (D&C 6:13; 14:7). The Church of Jesus Christ makes available the opportunity for worship, social growth, organized sacrifice, and receiving the ordinances of salvation. Salvation does not, however, come by the Church alone; it is the gospel of Christ that saves, as the gospel is the power of God unto salvation (Romans 1:16). Even with all the blessings appertaining to the Church, we could not be saved if there had been no atonement. No amount of effort on our part could compensate for the loss. The gift of salvation is in Christ, the Person.

*He shall grow up before him as a tender plant, and as a root out of
dry ground; he hath no form nor comeliness; and when we shall
see him there is no beauty that we should desire him.*

MOSIAH 14:2

Abinadi (quoting Isaiah) affirmed that the Messiah,
the King of kings, would not come to earth during his
mortal ministry in regal splendor, nor would he be
known by his good looks or his expensive clothing. In
almost all respects, the Son of God would engage mortality just as the rest of us do, and any advantages he
might have through being the Son of God would not
be obvious from his appearance alone. Jesus' divine
Sonship was known in the first century as it is known
today: by the quiet whisperings of the Holy Spirit.
Neither the power of his oratory nor the magnificence
of his miracles would be the principal means by which
people would know him. Rather, individuals of all ages
come to know Who he is and Whose he is through
personal revelation.

Yet it pleased the Lord to bruise him; he hath put him to grief;
when thou shalt make his soul an offering for sin he shall
see his seed, he shall prolong his days, and the pleasure
of the Lord shall prosper in his hand.

MOSIAH 14:10

Though in the strictest sense it did not please God the Father to witness the agony and suffering of his Son in the Garden and on the cross, the act of atonement was indeed central to the Father's plan for the salvation of his sons and daughters. It was absolutely necessary. Abinadi reminded his listeners, the priests of Noah, that when our Lord had accomplished his atoning work he would see his seed, enter that realm of disembodied spirits we know as paradise, and be welcomed by "an innumerable company of the spirits of the just," those "who had been faithful in the testimony of Jesus while they lived in mortality" (D&C 138:12). They were his seed in the sense that they had accepted the gospel covenant, been born again, and become his sons and daughters through regeneration; they were thereby heirs of the kingdom of God.

As ye are desirous to come into the fold of God, and to be called his people, and are willing to bear one another's burdens, . . . and to stand as witnesses of God at all times and in all things, . . . that ye may be redeemed of God, . . . ye may have eternal life.

MOSIAH 18:8–9

The Saints of God enter into the fold of his Church and thereby covenant to love and serve others. Although far from perfect, they are continually striving to improve, to put off the natural man, and become new creatures in Christ. But they are not self-focused. They bless and serve others in love; they give comfort to the downtrodden and empathy to the disheartened. True converts extend themselves to others; they reach out in kindness and compassion to fellow travelers on the road of life. The surest indication of their covenant relationship with Christ is how they lose themselves in helping others (Matthew 10:39). True religion is not practiced in some abstract, theoretical study of the doctrines of Christ. Pure religion is found in doing, in serving, in lifting others, and in witnessing through our actions that we are followers of Christ (James 1:27). May we be examples of the believers in word and deed (1 Timothy 4:12).

If this be the desire of your hearts, what have you against being baptized in the name of the Lord, as a witness before him that ye have entered into a covenant with him, that ye will serve him and keep his commandments, that he may pour out his Spirit more abundantly upon you?

MOSIAH 18:10

Baptism is essential unto salvation. The "first fruits of repentance" (Moroni 8:25), baptism is an outward sign of a sacred covenant, a two-way promise. When we are baptized, we covenant to bless others, keep the commandments, and stand as witnesses of God at all times. In return, God promises to pour out his Spirit upon us and redeem us from death. The spirit of the gospel is one of joy and good cheer. As righteous, covenant people, we need not have woeful countenances or be austere or ascetic. The gospel is the greatest message of gladness in the world! Those who follow Christ have buoyancy and hopefulness—despite the adversities and crucibles of life. No greater joy can bless our lives than to be "numbered with those of the first resurrection, that [we] may have eternal life" (Mosiah 18:9). This is God's great plan of happiness for us.

Ye shall not esteem one flesh above another, or one man shall not think himself above another; therefore I say unto you it is not expedient that ye should have a king.

MOSIAH 23:7

The people who fled with Alma into the wilderness loved him and wanted him to be their king. But Alma knew all too well what it was like to be subject to a wicked king. He taught them that if they could somehow ensure that the king would always be righteous, then it would be well for them to have a king. But there is no such guarantee. King Noah and his evil priests had ensnared the people in the bonds of iniquity, but now Alma and his faithful followers were free—free to stand fast in liberty, free to choose righteousness, free to reject evil and build the true church. Alma taught them that if they would remember the Lord, he would always deliver them (Mosiah 23). Just as Alma and his followers were rescued from King Noah, so may we too be delivered from ungodliness. The Lord will succor us in our sorrow and strengthen us in our trials if we come unto him.

Trust no one to be your teacher nor your minister, except he be a man of God, walking in his ways and keeping his commandments.
MOSIAH 23:14

We must be careful about those to whom we listen and choose to follow. Keeping our hands firmly on the iron rod, we must also keep our eyes riveted on the Lord's authorized servants: the First Presidency and the Quorum of the Twelve Apostles. Elder M. Russell Ballard taught: "Beware of those who speak and publish in opposition to God's true prophets and who actively proselyte others with reckless disregard for the eternal well-being of those whom they seduce. . . . in the Lord's Church there is no such thing as a 'loyal opposition.' One is either for the kingdom of God and stands in defense of God's prophets and apostles, or one stands opposed" (*Ensign*, November 1999, 63–64). The perilous times we live in and the even more perilous times ahead demand our continual vigilance and determination to follow the living prophets.

*Thus did Alma teach his people, that every man should
love his neighbor as himself, that there should be
no contention among them.*
MOSIAH 23:15

Driven into the wilderness by the people of King
Noah, Alma and his followers sought to live the gospel
fully. Alma taught that pure love is a fundamental
aspect of the everlasting covenant. More than a hundred
years later, during the Last Supper, Jesus would
instruct his apostles: "A new commandment I give
unto you, That ye love one another; as I have loved
you, that ye also love one another. By this shall all men
know that ye are my disciples, if ye have love one to
another" (John 13:34–35). From the beginning, the
Lord has taught his disciples to emphasize the importance
of loving one another, for love is essential to
having his Spirit and would stand as evidence that they
are true messengers of God. Everything about the
gospel of our Lord comes down to this vital teaching:
love one another.

*They were brought into bondage, and none could deliver
them but the Lord their God, yea,
even the God of Abraham and Isaac and of Jacob.*

MOSIAH 23:23

At one time or another, we find ourselves in the throes of bondage. Perhaps we become addicted to a substance or a lifestyle. Perhaps we are habituated to a sinful course. Perhaps we lose our freedom and find ourselves enslaved by enemies. There are, of course, many things we can do to break the shackles that bind us, no matter what our situation. In the end, however, only the Holy One of Israel can make us truly free— free from sin, free from behavioral patterns, free from ignorance, free from false traditions. The command in modern revelation is clear: "Abide ye in the liberty wherewith ye are made free; entangle not yourselves in sin, but let your hands be clean, until the Lord comes" (D&C 88:86). Further, "I, the Lord God, make you free, therefore ye are free indeed" (D&C 98:8). Only he who is the Truth can make us free (John 8:32).

*And it came to pass that the voice of the Lord
came to them in their afflictions.*

MOSIAH 24:13

If we were honest, we would admit that we desire to become more Christlike by navigating life with little toil, few barriers, and only one or two difficulties. That is, we yearn to join our Prototype at the top of the hill without being required to climb upwards. But the scriptures affirm that those who inherit the highest heaven are those who "overcome by faith" (D&C 76:53). The wise know firsthand that the most enduring lessons in life come in the furnace of affliction. When we are stripped of pride and double-mindedness, when we are naked in our frightening finitude, when as mortals we find ourselves up against the wall of faith, then is the time we open ourselves to the strength that comes only from him who knows perfectly how to succor his people (D&C 62:1). Eventually we cry out with the apostle Paul: "Most gladly therefore will I rather glory in my infirmities, that the power of Christ may rest upon me" (2 Corinthians 12:9).

JULY

*I, Nephi, beheld that the Gentiles
that had gone out of captivity were
delivered by the power of God out
of the hands of all other nations.*

1 NEPHI 13:19

I will also ease the burdens which are put upon your shoulders,
that even you cannot feel them upon your backs, . . . and
this will I do that ye may stand as witnesses for me hereafter,
and that ye may know of a surety that I, the Lord God,
do visit my people in their afflictions.

MOSIAH 24:14

Again and again God has miraculously delivered his people from suffering and even certain death. But holy writ also attests that he does not always do so. On many occasions he chooses to strengthen us in the midst of our troubles rather than remove us from them. There are lessons to be learned, experience to be acquired, compassion and empathy to be developed through suffering. James wrote: "My brethren, count it all joy when ye fall into many afflictions; knowing this, that the trying of your faith worketh patience. But let patience have her perfect work that ye may be perfect and entire, wanting nothing" (JST James 1:2–4). To be sure, few of us would pray for trials, for trials come into our lives without our invitation. At the same time, an elevated perspective upon our difficulties will aid us in our understanding of how God is making us more and more like him. We are then able to bear witness of the power of deliverance that comes into our lives through seeking after the Holy One of Israel.

Notwithstanding there being many churches they were all one
church, yea, even the church of God; for there was
nothing preached in all the churches except
it were repentance and faith in God.
MOSIAH 25:22.

A challenge we face as members of the restored Church is to teach the doctrines of salvation and at the same time keep the doctrine pure. The slightest deviation in doctrinal meaning can lead to enormous difficulties and unspeakable tragedy. We are only saved to the extent that we believe the truth and abide by that truth; no amount of sincerity or enthusiasm for a false precept will lead us to God. Thus we are encouraged to teach "none other things than that which the prophets and apostles have written, and that which is taught them by the Comforter through the prayer of faith" (D&C 52:9). The leaders of the Church, both local and general, travel throughout the Church and visit the branches and wards to see to it that what is being taught is in harmony with the teachings of the living oracles and thus with the mind and will of the Almighty.

*There were many of the rising generation that could not under-
stand the words of king Benjamin, being little children at the
time he spake unto his people; and they did not believe the
tradition of their fathers. And now because of
their unbelief . . . their hearts were hardened.*

MOSIAH 26:1, 3

A believing heart is surely one of the great gifts of
the Spirit. There are some things a cynic can never
understand, some things a skeptic can never comprehend, some things a doubter can never appreciate. As
Bryant S. Hinckley taught his son, "Cynics do not contribute, skeptics do not create, doubters do not
achieve" (Hinckley, *Way to Be*, 84). No one is called
upon to be gullible or to follow blindly; rather, we are
called upon to be open, humble, teachable, and receptive to new truth. We are thus counseled by the Lord
to "search diligently, pray always, and be believing, and
all things shall work together for your good, if ye walk
uprightly and remember the covenant wherewith ye
have covenanted one with another" (D&C 90:24).

Alma . . . inquired of the Lord what he should do concerning this matter, for he feared that he should do wrong in the sight of God. And . . . after he had poured out his whole soul to God, the voice of the Lord came to him.

MOSIAH 26:13–14

It is not uncommon for us to feel inadequate in working with the souls of the children of men. This is as it ought to be, for we are inadequate, at least on our own. It is a sobering matter to strive to lead another person to Christ and not make a mistake in the process. But we need not yield to the natural tendency to feel overwhelmed, for this is the work of the Lord, and he knows what to do. Ours is a divine investiture of authority, a solemn commission to act on his behalf and to say and do what he would say and do if he personally were ministering among us. Such direction, such specific instruction comes to us just as it came to Alma: After we have poured out our whole soul to God, the voice of the Lord will come to us, offer reassurance, and make known what actions to take. What a comfort for our feelings of inadequacy!

Thou art my servant; and I covenant with thee that thou shalt have eternal life; and thou shalt serve me and go forth in my name, and shalt gather together my sheep.

MOSIAH 26:20

Alma was blessed to receive a lengthy directive on how to deal with transgressors, the details of which are especially helpful today as we strive to lead the prodigal back to the fold. In the midst of the divine instructions to Alma on this difficult matter is God's covenant with his servant that he (Alma) will have eternal life. Alma was not on a spiritual crusade, nor was he seeking to be truer than true. He was not spiritually unbalanced, was not on a personal campaign to make his calling and election sure. Instead, he was simply going about the work to which he'd been called, laboring tirelessly in behalf of his brothers and sisters. There is a message there for us. In the words of President Joseph F. Smith, "To do well those things which God ordained to be the common lot of all mankind, is the truest greatness" (*Gospel Doctrine*, 285).

The sons of Mosiah were numbered among the unbelievers;
and also one of the sons of Alma was numbered among them. . . .
And he was a man of many words, and did speak much
flattery to the people; therefore he led many of the
people to do after the manner of his iniquities.

MOSIAH 27:8

We can only imagine Alma's heartache and embarrassment in overseeing the kingdom and regulating the Church when his son and the sons of King Mosiah were actively seeking to block the progress of the Church. There were likely many sleepless nights and much anguish of soul felt by the parents of those wayward young men. As is often the case, these parents probably engaged in long periods of introspection, wondering where they had fallen short and what they could have done differently. It must have been extremely difficult for Alma and Mosiah to stand before large congregations and invite families to unite in the gospel cause while their own posterity were wreaking havoc among the Saints. But to their everlasting credit, the parents never gave up; the prayers of the parents and the pleadings of the members of the Church ascended to that God who acknowledges and responds to the "effectual fervent prayer of [the] righteous" (James 5:16).

*All mankind, yea, men and women, all nations, kindreds, tongues
and people, must be born again; yea, born of God, changed from
their carnal and fallen state, to a state of righteousness,
being redeemed of God, . . . and unless they do this,
they can in nowise inherit the kingdom of God.*

MOSIAH 27:25–26

The gospel of Jesus Christ is intended to do more than make bad men good and good men better, although it certainly does that. The gospel "is the power of God unto salvation" (Romans 1:16). God is in the business of change, and his plan of salvation is intended to change the crowning creature of his creations. As a result of the Fall, we find ourselves alienated from God and his righteousness, dead to the things of the Spirit. The call for all humankind to be born again is as old as the world (Moses 6:58–60), a call to come unto Christ and open ourselves to the Savior's transforming power. To be born again is to become a new creature of Christ, a new creation of the Holy Ghost; it is to be transformed from darkness to light, from a heart bent on evil deeds to a soul that delights in the things of God.

*They traveled throughout all the land of Zarahemla, . . . zealously
striving to repair all the injuries which they had done to the
church. . . . And thus they were instruments in the hands
of God in bringing many to the knowledge of the truth. . . .
how blessed are they!*

MOSIAH 27:35–37

Alma and the sons of Mosiah had experienced a
mighty change. Now, as new creatures in Christ, they
earnestly tried to repair the damage they had done and
humbly confessed the error of their ways. Their con-
versions engendered persecution, perhaps from
former friends and apostates who disbelieved the sincerity of their change and wanted to remain in rebellion, wickedness, and indolence. Nevertheless, these
young converts were now different, forever changed,
transformed from the natural man to the Saint who
suffers much, keeps the commandments, witnesses
unto others of the loving kindness of God, and
declares unto one and all that salvation is in Jesus the
Christ (Mosiah 27:32–37). True believers want others
to experience a mighty change; they desire that others
will feel the peace of righteousness. How blessed are
they who are converted and who help others come
unto Christ.

*Now they were desirous that salvation should be declared to every
creature, for they could not bear that any human soul should
perish. . . . And thus did the Spirit of the Lord work upon
them, for they were the very vilest of sinners.*

MOSIAH 28:3–4

Once individuals have been transformed by the pure love of Christ, they automatically turn their attention to the welfare of others. Because they have been lifted and liberated, they desire the same for all of God's children. Because they have been cleansed and renewed, they hope for the regeneration of all their brothers and sisters. Alma and the sons of Mosiah having faced an early judgment and felt the bitter pangs associated with seeing things as they really are, their deepest yearning was to assist others to avoid such a consummate confrontation. The mercy of God had snatched vile sinners from their perverse path, and now these sinners, fully repentant and forgiven, sought to become messengers of mercy to everyone they encountered.

It is better that a man should be judged of God than of man,
for the judgments of God are always just, but the
judgments of man are not always just.
MOSIAH 29:12

Even the best of people can make mistakes in judgment. Because our vision is limited and we can never fully know the thoughts and intents of another, our judgments are finite and often less than perfect. How reassuring to know that there is One who looks on the heart (1 Samuel 16:7), One whose judgments are merciful yet just, One who knows the beginning and the end—and everything in between. We can trust our righteous judge (Moses 6:57) because he is perfect and his judgments are flawless. The words of Abinadi echo down the centuries, "The time shall come when all shall see the salvation of the Lord; when every nation, kindred, tongue, and people shall see eye to eye and shall confess before God that his judgments are just" (Mosiah 16:1). Perfect judgment is the province alone of him who is perfect.

If the time comes that the voice of the people doth choose iniquity,
then is the time that the judgments of God will come upon you;
yea, then is the time he will visit you with great destruction
even as he has hitherto visited this land.

MOSIAH 29:27

Though it is clear that many in our day have turned a deaf ear to the commandments of God and the words of living prophets, there are still many who love the Lord and live their lives according to the time-honored values that make nations great. We are to be cautious and vigilant regarding the erosion of moral values, but we must also maintain that quiet optimism that characterizes a people who know that in the end the victory is the Lord's. The "voice of the people" need not be a majority, however. Our concern must not be only that good people outnumber bad people. It is possible, because of the complacency of otherwise good people who refuse to step forward and stand up for morality and decency, that the voice of a minority whose motives are malevolent and whose intent is evil can become in effect the voice of the people.

He also testified unto the people that all mankind should be saved
at the last day, and that they need not fear nor tremble, . . .
for the Lord had created all men, and had also redeemed
all men; and, in the end, all men should have eternal life.
ALMA 1:4

Nephi had warned of the evils of priestcraft, the effort to preach the gospel for material gain or popularity (2 Nephi 26:29). The antichrist Nehor bore down against the Church, encouraging priests and teachers to become popular and look to the people for their support. He taught that because everyone would be saved at the last day, it was not necessary for people to fear God or feel guilty for their sins: There was no need for repentance, because all would eventually have eternal life (Alma 15:15; 21:8). Like other antichrists, he denied the spirit of prophecy and revelation. Being oblivious to the things of eternity and thus "past feeling" (1 Nephi 17:45), he complicated his priestcraft with murder and thereafter died a shameful death. What Nehor lacked was the spiritual ingredient that is the antidote to priestcraft, the preventative measure against apostasy and hardness of heart, as well as the impetus for establishing Zion—he lacked charity (2 Nephi 26:30–31).

*There were many among them who began to be proud, and began
to contend warmly with their adversaries. . . . yea, it was the cause
of much trial with the church. For the hearts of many were
hardened, and their names were blotted out, that they were
remembered no more among the people of God.*

ALMA 1:22–24

A hard lesson for us to learn is that whenever we
engage in argument or debate about sacred things,
we are wrong. Even if our message is right and true, we
are wrong. Persuasion and conversion to the truth
come only through the quiet whisperings of the Holy
Spirit (1 Corinthians 2:11–14), not through intellectual jangling or overmuch logic. It is possible for a
faithful member of the Church to become, essentially,
anti-anti in their response to others who oppose our
faith. In the process the Church member forfeits the
right to the gift of the Holy Ghost and places himself
in spiritual peril. The risen Lord taught the Nephites
that "he that hath the spirit of contention is not of me,
but is of the devil, who is the father of contention, and
he stirreth up the hearts of men to contend with
anger, one with another" (3 Nephi 11:29). We do not
debate. We teach and we testify.

*Thus, in their prosperous circumstances, . . . they did not set
their hearts upon riches; therefore they were liberal to all, both
old and young, both bond and free, both male and female,
whether out of the church or in the church, having no
respect to persons as to those who stood in need.*

ALMA 1:30

The Savior taught that as we serve one of the least of our brothers and sisters, we serve him (Matthew 25:40). Likewise, King Benjamin observed that the simplest way to serve God is to serve the children of God (Mosiah 2:17). The revelations of the Restoration attest to the universal Fatherhood of God and the brotherhood of man. Though our natural tendency is to look to the needs of those within the household of faith, the divine directive is that our love and caring should extend beyond the bounds of the organization of the Church. The Prophet Joseph Smith taught that "love is one of the chief characteristics of Deity, and ought to be manifested by those who aspire to be the sons of God. A man filled with the love of God is not content with blessing his family alone, but ranges through the whole world, anxious to bless the whole human race" (*Teachings*, 174).

Alma, being a man of God, being exercised with much faith, cried, saying: O Lord, have mercy and spare my life, that I may be an instrument in thy hands to save and preserve this people.

ALMA 2:30

In the midst of battle with the wicked and cunning Amlici, Alma offered a prayer. Not the petition of one terrified by the possibility of death, his was the pleading of a worthy man who regularly conversed with his Father. Alma's life was in order, and his prayer was a prayer of faith. His confidence was in his Lord. Wanting to safeguard his people, his earnest desires were neither selfish nor out of harmony with divine will. Indeed, he was strengthened in his man-to-man struggle with Amlici and slew him. Likewise, we are buoyed up in our battles and fortified in our faith as we sincerely pray for heaven's help, as we live worthy of divine assistance, as our requests are selfless and in submission to God's will. Whether we are stressed by the mundane matters of this world or challenged by greater adversities, we must turn to the Lord and put our trust in him.

*The people of the church began to be lifted up in the pride of their
eyes, and to set their hearts upon riches and upon the vain things
of the world, that they began to be scornful, one towards
another. . . . yea, there were envyings, and strife,
and malice, and persecutions, and pride.*

ALMA 4:8–9

Of all people, members of the Lord's Church
should be humble, to know whence their blessings
come and in whom they must trust for salvation. If
Saints—whether they be latter-day or yesteryear—are
severely afflicted with pride, they are not, in the truest
sense, Saints. When a person wastes energy looking
down on others rather than looking up to Christ, he
will grieve the Spirit of Christ and thus alienate the
very power by which relationships are sweetened and
sustained. Rather than being filled with kindhearted-
ness, humility, and gratitude, a proud person is filled
with resentment, enmity, and discontent. Rather than
extending service and friendship, he selfishly with-
holds time, talents, and means that could bless
another. True believers are called out of the world into
the marvelous light of Christ (1 Peter 2:9). True Saints
beware of pride as they humbly reach out to others in
love.

*Thus ended the eighth year of the reign of the judges; and the
wickedness of the church was a great stumbling-block to
those who did not belong to the church; and thus the
church began to fail in its progress.*

ALMA 4:10

The God of heaven works his wonders in mysterious ways. The Omniscient One does so through people, ordinary people like ourselves, the weak things of the earth (D&C 1:19). The strength of the Church lies not alone in the power of the witness borne by apostles and prophets. Rather, the strength of the Church, including its ability to grow and expand and affect the larger world, is in the witness and evident faithfulness of its members. No man is an island, and there are no private sins. Thus what I do as an individual affects more than just myself and even those closest to me; it affects, as it were, the entire Church. As the Master ministered one by one, so the progress of the Church takes place as faithful individuals contribute to the health and vitality of the body of Christ.

This he did that he himself . . . might preach the word of God unto them, to stir them up in remembrance of their duty, and that he might pull down, by the word of God, all the pride and craftiness and all the contentions which were among his people.

ALMA 4:19

Faith comes "by hearing, and hearing by the word of God" (Romans 10:17). Indeed, "faith comes by hearing the word of God, through the testimony of the servants of God; that testimony is always attended by the Spirit of prophecy and revelation" (Smith, *Teachings*, 148). There is power, amazing power associated with the bearing of pure testimony, which is more than a public offering of thanks, an acknowledgment of God's goodness, or an expression of love for family, as important as such declarations are. People bear pure testimony when they bear witness of the reality of God, of the divine Sonship of Christ, of the prophetic call of Joseph Smith and his successors, of the truthfulness of the Book of Mormon and of modern revelation, and of the divinity of the living Church. Further, speakers and teachers bear pure testimony when they are able to bear solemn witness that what they have taught is true. Such testimony influences human souls. Such testimony changes the world.

Behold, I ask of you, my brethren of the church,
have ye spiritually been born of God? Have ye received
his image in your countenances? Have ye experienced
this mighty change in your hearts?
ALMA 5:14

Alma taught the Zoramites that "every seed bringeth forth unto its own likeness" (Alma 32:31). Those who have been born again, who have become the sons and daughters of Jesus Christ by adoption, take upon them the family name and are expected to bear that name with fidelity and devotion. In addition, they begin to acquire the Christlike attributes that characterize the Father of their salvation—they bear the image of the Son of God. Those whose hearts have been changed by the Master not only begin to emulate their Master but to reflect the character and benevolence and divine love that entice others to greater righteousness.

If ye have experienced a change of heart, and if ye have felt to sing the song of redeeming love, I would ask, can ye feel so now?
ALMA 5:26

P raise ye the Lord: for it is good to sing praises unto our God" (Psalm 147:1). Who has not felt to sing songs of thanksgiving for blessings from a generous God? Surely all within the household of faith desire to express love and acknowledge the greatness of our Heavenly Father and his Only Begotten Son. The Lord said, "For my soul delighteth in the song of the heart; yea, the song of the righteous is a prayer unto me, and it shall be answered with a blessing upon their heads" (D&C 25:12). Songs of heavenly praise help sanctify and cleanse our souls. And when our hearts are truly changed, we want to sing songs of praise and worship continually. We can't rest on our laurels, however. Whatever our service and commitment have been in the past, we are still needed today. Our task is to continue, to move forward with faith, to progress— all the while singing the song of redeeming love.

He will take upon him death, that he may loose the bands of
death which bind his people; and he will take upon him their
infirmities, that his bowels may be filled with mercy, . . .
that he may know according to the flesh how to succor
his people according to their infirmities.

ALMA 7:12

Jesus did not have to die. As the Son of the Eternal Father, he possessed the powers of immortality and could have remained alive. Instead, he offered himself into the hands of his enemies and, of his own free will, yielded his mortal life. In the most profound expression of love, he suffered and died and then rose from the tomb. His offering was voluntary (John 10:17–18). His sacrifice completely satisfied the law. Not only did he deliver us from sin and death but he also took upon himself our infirmities and sorrows. What can we tell him about suffering that he does not understand? No pain that we experience can be separated from the love of Christ, who, in a manner incomprehensible to us, took upon him our collective and individual anguish and heartache. Christ knows; he fully understands. We can be comforted and consoled in Christ, who is filled with perfect empathy, mercy, and love for each one of us.

*See that ye have faith, hope, and charity, and then ye
will always abound in good works.*

ALMA 7:24

Sometimes we tend to get the cart before the horse.
One who has true faith in Christ trusts in him, has confidence in his atoning power, and learns to rely upon
his merits and mercy and grace. Hope is the anticipation, the expectation, and the assurance of eternal life
through Christ. We experience charity as the Lord
accepts our repentance and grants unto us a remission
of sins. Truly, "this love which [Jesus] hast had for the
children of men is charity; wherefore, except men shall
have charity they cannot inherit that place which thou
hast prepared in the mansions of thy Father" (Ether
12:34). These three spiritual endowments—perhaps the
greatest of all (1 Corinthians 13:13)—rightly precede
the performance of good works. When our lives have
been surrendered to the Captain of our souls and when
our hearts have been renewed and empowered through
his loving atonement, the works of righteousness follow naturally.

An angel of the Lord appeared unto him, saying: Blessed art thou,
Alma; therefore, lift up thy head and rejoice . . . for thou hast
been faithful in keeping the commandments of God from the time
which thou receivedst thy first message from him.
ALMA 8:14–15

The same angel who struck down wayward Alma and
the sons of Mosiah two decades earlier (Mosiah 27;
Alma 36) returned to console and direct this now-
faithful servant of God (Alma 8:15–17). The angel
assured Alma that his offering was acceptable to the
Lord, despite the wickedness of those he taught. Many
of us have felt like Alma at times, weighed down with
heartache because of the bad choices of someone we
love. Comfort comes as we turn heavenward in prayer.
Our burdens are lifted as we turn to the Savior. Indeed,
peace of soul, an inner assurance that God is pleased
with our best efforts, comes to the obedient and faithful
that is unknown to the fickle and uncommitted. Such
feelings come despite lack of success, according to our
finite perspective, in attaining worthy goals we have set.
No matter the outcome, those who labor with fidelity
and devotion, seeking diligently to lead others to Christ
and his kingdom, are successful in the Lord's eyes.

*Thou art a holy prophet of God, for thou art the man whom an
angel said in a vision: Thou shalt receive. Therefore, go with
me into my house and I will impart unto thee of my food;
and I know that thou wilt be a blessing unto me.*
ALMA 8:20

Divine providence orchestrates a way for the kingdom to roll forth. Of great importance is the care and
keeping of the Lord's anointed. What a privilege to shel-
ter and attend to the servants of God. Their presence
and spiritual power prove an unspeakable blessing to the
homes in which they visit. Imagine hosting a prophet of
God in your home. Would he be comfortable with the
spirit there? Would he want to linger, or quickly leave?
Would he, like Alma, bless you and your family? (Alma
8:22). Mormon's account indicates that "Alma tarried
many days with Amulek before he began to preach unto
the people" (Alma 8:27). What a remarkable experience
it must have been to be tutored and prepared by Alma
and by angels before their missionary journeyings
(Alma 10:10). Amulek's home, during this brief season,
was a kind of missionary training center—which is
exactly what our homes are: a place of training and
preparation for faithful followers of Christ.

I was called many times and I would not hear; therefore I knew concerning these things, yet I would not know; therefore I went on rebelling against God, in the wickedness of my heart.

ALMA 10:6

The voice of the Lord calls to us regularly. Often, it is not sin that dulls our minds and hearts to spiritual impressions. Wickedness and carnality are not the only things that keep us from feeling and hearing the word. The problem may be simply that our minds and hearts are focused upon other things. We may be so caught up in the cares of the world, so busy being busy, that we crowd out the sweet whisperings of the Spirit. We become so involved in the thick of thin things that we don't take time to listen to the words of the living prophets, ponder the things of eternity, or supplicate our Maker in sincere prayer. Excessive concentration on secondary matters can block spiritual opportunities that flow naturally when we place primary attention on everlasting things. We must not live in the twilight beneath our spiritual privileges but, with softened hearts and listening ears, bask in the glory of the noonday Son.

O ye wicked and perverse generation, why hath Satan got such
great hold upon your hearts? Why will ye yield yourselves
unto him that he may have power over you, to blind
your eyes, that ye will not understand the words
which are spoken, according to their truth?

ALMA 10:25

The father of all lies became the devil because he sought to destroy the agency of man; his very reason for being is to deceive and blind us, to lead us captive at his will (Moses 4:3–5). What great injury comes to us when we ascribe evil to that which is good, and good to that which is evil. "Satan has had great success with this gullible generation," said Elder James E. Faust. "There is, however, an ample shield against the power of Lucifer and his hosts. This protection lies in the spirit of discernment through the gift of the Holy Ghost. This gift comes undeviatingly by personal revelation to those who strive to obey the commandments of the Lord" (*Ensign,* November 1987, 35–36). If we are in tune, the light of the Spirit will help us reject evil and all its subtleties and embrace that which is good.

He said unto Amulek: Will ye answer the questions which I shall put unto you? And Amulek said unto him: Yea, if it be according to the Spirit of the Lord, which is in me; for I shall say nothing which is contrary to the Spirit of the Lord.

ALMA 11:21–22

Although we are eager to proclaim the gospel of Jesus Christ and spread the good news of salvation to all the world, we cannot answer every question that arises in the minds of people. Some questions are simply unanswerable because God has not revealed an answer. In other cases, it is clear that the questioner has ulterior motives and is seeking to trap us. It is then that we would do well to teach the truth simply, bear testimony, and move on. Whatever the circumstance, however, we should follow the example of Amulek, who taught us that our natural inclination to respond to questions should be inextricably linked to the spiritual prompting to do so. Surely, no one would want to venture into deeper waters or enter into a conversation unless it was approved of the Lord. We thus strive to cultivate the spirit of inspiration not only to know what answer to give but whether it should be given at all.

Zeezrom said: Is there more than one God? And he answered,
No. And Zeezrom said again: Who is he that shall come?
Is it the Son of God? And he said unto him, Yea.
ALMA 11:28–29, 32–33

The crafty lawyer Zeezrom encountered a holy man of God, one who knew the gospel is true and, just as important, knew the gospel. The Book of Mormon is a monumental testimony of Jesus the Christ. He is its central character. Amulek was perfectly aware of the reality of God our Heavenly Father, but he and Alma had been speaking primarily of the coming of the Son of God to earth as our Mediator and Redeemer. As Abinadi pointed out, Jesus will be both Father and Son, both God and man (Mosiah 15:1–4). Only through having inherited mortality from his mother, Mary, could our Lord fully comprehend the sorrows and sicknesses and challenges and infirmities and temptations of man. Only by possessing the powers of immortality from his immortal Father could Jesus have had the capacity to bear the unbearable and later take up his body in a glorious resurrection. Thus, Jesus was God, and he was also the Son of God.

This restoration shall come to all, both old and young, both bond and free, both male and female, both the wicked and the righteous; and even there shall not so much as a hair of their heads be lost; but every thing shall be restored to its perfect frame.

ALMA 11:44

Resurrected immortality is a free gift. It comes to us as an unconditional blessing of the Atonement. "All your losses will be made up to you in the resurrection," the Prophet Joseph Smith explained, "provided you continue faithful. By the vision of the Almighty, I have seen it" (*Teachings*, 296). The Latter-day Saints, and all other Christians for that matter, find supernal peace in the assurance of the immortality of the soul, in the certain expectation that death is not the end, that life and learning and love span the veil of death. Further, we shall retain our identity and be reunited with our loved ones in an unbroken genealogical chain that continues back to Adam. We cry out with the apostle Paul, "O death, where is thy sting? O grave, where is thy victory? But thanks be to God, which giveth us the victory through our Lord Jesus Christ" (1 Corinthians 15:55, 57).

He that will harden his heart, the same receiveth the lesser portion of the word; and he that will not harden his heart, to him is given the greater portion of the word, until it is given unto him to know the mysteries of God until he know them in full.

ALMA 12:10

If any of you lack wisdom, let him ask of God, that giveth to all men liberally, and upbraideth not; and it shall be given him" (James 1:5). "Ask, and it shall be given you; seek, and ye shall find; knock, and it shall be opened unto you: for everyone that asketh receiveth; and he that seeketh findeth; and to him that knocketh it shall be opened" (Matthew 7:7–8). No divine directive is more prominent in scripture than the Lord's simple invitation for us to ask. Alma taught that those who close themselves to further light and knowledge, who have the attitude of "we have received, and we need no more" (2 Nephi 28:27) suffer the consequences of their spiritual indifference: they gain no more. On the other hand, those who with patient maturity seek to grow in light and truth, line upon line and precept upon precept, will receive the greater portion of the word and thereby know the mysteries of God.

Our words will condemn us, yea, all our works will condemn us;
. . . and our thoughts will also condemn us; and in this awful state
we shall not dare to look up to our God; and we would fain be glad
if we could command the rocks and the mountains to fall upon us.

ALMA 12:14

If we truly seek to come unto Christ, we must be willing to improve in every aspect. Much like going to a dentist, we may have acute pain around one tooth and want it to be fixed. But in the process, the dentist finds other decay that needs treatment as well. There may not be pain elsewhere yet, but he advises prevention and outlines a treatment plan. Likewise, the Great Physician beckons us to forsake sin and turn our lives over to him, to receive treatment not just for actions that warrant correction but also for words and thoughts. None of us is perfect—we err in judgments and speak or do or think what we should not. But if our desires are to be like and with God and we repent speedily (D&C 109:21), then when we place our wills on the altar and offer all that we have, we can be transformed by the Lord's loving hand and be found spotless at the last day.

AUGUST

*He shall go forth, suffering pains
and afflictions and temptations of
every kind; and this that the word
might be fulfilled which saith he
will take upon him the pains and
the sicknesses of his people.*

ALMA 7:11

*Therefore God gave unto them commandments, after having
made known unto them the plan of redemption, that they should
not do evil, the penalty thereof being a second death, . . .
for the works of justice could not be destroyed,
according to the supreme goodness of God.*

ALMA 12:32

The gospel of Jesus Christ is not merely a system of ethics, although it certainly embodies rules of proper conduct and behavior. The plan of salvation is foundational to all that we do—and refrain from doing. We teach the principles of salvation and then may speak of proper conduct. Ethics must be grounded in doctrine if they are to escape the moral erosion of a decaying society. "True doctrine, understood, changes attitudes and behavior," Elder Boyd K. Packer observed. "The study of the doctrines of the gospel will improve behavior quicker than a study of behavior will improve behavior. . . . That is why we stress so forcefully the study of the doctrines of the gospel" (*Ensign,* November 1986, 17). Ours must be a confidence in the power of the word of God to touch and transform the sons and daughters of God, a power greater "than the sword, or anything else" (Alma 31:5).

They have been called to this holy calling on account of their faith, while others would reject the Spirit of God on account of the hardness of their hearts and blindness of their minds, while, if it had not been for this they might have had as great privilege as their brethren.

ALMA 13:4

Though it is true that we once lived in the presence of God and heard from his lips the plan of salvation declared, it was necessary that faith be exercised in him and his plan. Those who exercised "exceedingly great faith" in the premortal realm bring with them into mortality a predisposition to recognize and accept the truth when it is presented (Alma 13:3). But their faith in this life must be such that they hearken to the invitation of the Spirit of God to come into the gospel covenant. If, instead, they harden their hearts to the message of salvation, they forfeit blessings and privileges that might have been theirs had they remained faithful. In a sense, then, many were called and foreordained in the premortal world to a great and noble calling in this life, but if they do not live up to their spiritual opportunities, they are not counted among the chosen. Chosenness is always a product of proper choices.

Now they, after being sanctified by the Holy Ghost, having their garments made white, being pure and spotless before God, could not look upon sin save it were with abhorrence; and there were many, exceedingly great many, who were made pure and entered into the rest of the Lord their God.

ALMA 13:12

Alma described for us a valuable pattern of conversion. Once individuals have received a remission of sins and been "washed white through the blood of the Lamb" (Alma 13:11)—that is, sanctified or cleansed by the Spirit—their hearts begin to change and their behaviors are automatically affected. They begin to hate the things that they before loved and to love the things that they before hated. They are drawn and enticed toward God, godliness, and the praiseworthy things of this world. Having tasted the sweet fruits of salvation, they are repulsed by influences that degrade and distort. Once one has entered the realm of divine experience and basked in the light of true Sainthood, this world's paltry offerings are seen for what they are: fleeting, futile, and finite.

*Humble yourselves before the Lord, and call on his holy name,
and watch and pray continually, that ye may not be tempted
above that which ye can bear, and thus be led by the
Holy Spirit, becoming humble, meek, submissive,
patient, full of love and all long-suffering.*

ALMA 13:28

Those led by the Spirit try to stay far away from the
precipice of temptation and sin. They do not flirt with
spiritual dangers or think they are strong enough to
withstand sudden gusts of adversarial wind. Faithful
Saints are always watchful as they call upon the Lord to
help them resist the enticements of the world. They are
meek and humble followers of Christ who find safety
in holy places. Blessed with buoyancy, even cheerful-
ness, they seek to be filled with God's love. "Saints do
not have sad or woeful countenances," wrote Elder
Neal A. Maxwell. "They are much more interesting
than sinners. Sinners are so much the same in their
sadness. Sometimes their very flamboyance betrays
their sense of sameness" (*Quote Book*, 293). As we put off
the natural man and exercise faith, hope, and charity,
we will be blessed with the fruit of the Spirit, come to
know the soul satisfaction of righteousness, and be
numbered among the household of Saints.

Having faith on the Lord; having a hope that ye shall receive eternal life; having the love of God always in your hearts, that ye may be lifted up at the last day and enter into his rest.

ALMA 13:29

Faith, hope, and charity pave the path of peace. These gifts of the Spirit bring joy in this life and eternal glory in the world to come. In the end, it is not the mysteries of the kingdom that save us nor, necessarily, the profound, deep doctrines that change our hearts. Alma concluded his great sermon by reviewing the fundamentals of Sainthood: *faith* unto life and salvation that centers in the Lord and his atoning sacrifice and resurrection; *hope* that rests in the Savior, who makes repentance, forgiveness, immortality and eternal life possible; and *charity,* or pure love of Christ, that is manifest in us and is perhaps the surest indication of our striving for Saintliness. We can enter into the rest of the Lord, here and hereafter, by sincerely having faith in Jesus, hope in eternal life, and charity for one another.

The Spirit constraineth me that I must not stretch forth mine hand; for behold the Lord receiveth them up unto himself, in glory; and he doth suffer that they may do this thing . . . that the judgments which he shall exercise upon them in his wrath may be just.

ALMA 14:11

The Lord has had the power to change all events from the beginning, but, as he stated, "My thoughts are not your thoughts, neither are your ways my ways, saith the Lord" (Isaiah 55:8). God is never the source of evil, yet within limits and laws he allows evil to exist in order to bring about his purposes. Because we live in a world of opposition, the righteous can merit the fulness of his glory and the wicked can inherit the fulness of his wrath. Evil actions condemn the wicked and will be remembered as a witness against them at the coming day of judgment, while suffering sanctifies the souls of the faithful and prepares them to live with the Lord in glory. Our loving God, who is mindful of all persons, has witnessed all forms of suffering—he "having provided some better things for them through their sufferings, for without sufferings they could not be made perfect" (JST Hebrews 11:40). By trusting in the Lord and his ways, we enter into his glory.

*Alma said: Be it according to the will of the Lord. But,
behold, our work is not finished;
therefore they burn us not.*

ALMA 14:13

As with Alma and Abinadi of old, and Joseph Smith in our dispensation, righteous servants are preserved until their mission is complete. Workers of iniquity have no power to slay those of the household of faith until they have fulfilled their divine callings (Mosiah 13:7; D&C 122:9). When the Lord issues a call, he sends the powers of heaven to preserve and protect and strengthen his willing servants. He who knows when the sparrow falls also knows how many days each of us is allotted. No wicked design can cut short our appointed days, especially for those on the Lord's errand. Those who have consecrated their lives to the will of God can go forward with faith as they accomplish their life's mission. We must trust the Lord and his will for us.

Alma cried unto the Lord, saying: O Lord our God, have mercy on this man, and heal him according to his faith which is in Christ.
ALMA 15:10

Our faith unto salvation, our faith to heal and be healed, rests in the Savior, not in the officiator of a blessing. The account of Zeezrom affirms this truth and illustrates how the physical and the spiritual are inseparably connected. Some physical ailments have their roots in spiritual maladies. The tentacles of guilt descend to the depth of the human heart to do immeasurable damage to the soul. Zeezrom was sick with the reality of his wickedness and tormented with remorse. He desired Alma and Amulek to heal him, which they did after inquiring about his faith in Christ. His repentance was sincere, his conversion complete as he was healed and then baptized by Alma. He proved his great faith by serving as a devoted missionary companion with those who had brought him the gospel (Alma 15:1–12). Indeed, the changing power that is in Christ can work mighty miracles of the soul.

They had searched the scriptures diligently, that they might know the word of God. But this is not all; they had given themselves to much prayer, and fasting; therefore they had the spirit of prophecy, and the spirit of revelation, and when they taught, they taught with power and authority of God.

ALMA 17:2–3

Sincere prayer, fasting, and scripture study are sure passports to spiritual power. This grand triumvirate—earnest prayer, fasting, and scripture study—opens the door to repentance and forgiveness as well as helps us to become worthy instruments in the hands of God (Alma 17:9). Spiritual sustenance of this kind strengthens us for the challenges of life and is a way to manifest our humble devotion to God (Alma 17:11). Alma and the sons of Mosiah had known the emptiness of wickedness, but now, as courageous missionaries for the Lord, they had stepped from darkness into light and wanted to share the great plan of happiness with all people. Although they had experienced a mighty change of heart, prayer, fasting, and scripture study were vital to maintaining their spiritual posture. Consecrated life in the Lord requires a regular process of spiritual strengthening.

*Now Ammon being wise, yet harmless, he said unto Lamoni:
Wilt thou hearken unto my words, if I tell thee by what power I
do these things? And this is the thing that I desire of thee. And the
king answered him, and said: Yea, I will believe all thy words.*

ALMA 18:22—23

Joseph Smith taught that it is one thing to be born
again to see the kingdom of God and another thing to
be born again to enter therein (*Teachings,* 328).
Individuals are born again to see the kingdom of God
when they recognize the servants of the Lord for who
they are: ambassadors of the Prince of Peace and messengers of glory. As the Spirit of the Lord begins to
work upon the heart of investigators, the barriers of
cynicism and skepticism flee and the individual devel-
ops a believing heart. In the list of spiritual gifts given
in modern revelation, the first gift named is the gift of
testimony, the gift of knowing that Jesus Christ is the
Son of God and that he was crucified for the sins of
the world. Interestingly enough, the next gift named
is the gift to believe on the words of those who know,
"that they also might have eternal life if they continue
faithful" (D&C 46:14).

He knew that king Lamoni was under the power of God; . . .
yea, this light had infused such joy into his soul, the cloud
of darkness having been dispelled, and that the light of
everlasting life was lit up in his soul.

ALMA 19:6

King Lamoni embraced the light of everlasting life. His experience is a marvelous account of the conversion process, a process universal to all who choose the light of the gospel over the darkness of unbelief. Elder Henry B. Eyring taught, "God our Heavenly Father has given us the right to know the truth. He has shown that the way to receive that truth is simple, so simple that a child can follow it. Once it is followed, more light comes from God to enlighten the understanding of His faithful spirit child. . . . A foundation built on truth and illuminated by the light of God will free us from the fear that we might be overcome" (*Ensign,* July 2001, 13). Scriptures use *light* and *truth* interchangeably. God is light. God is truth. Truth sanctifies (John 17:17); light and truth forsake that which is evil (D&C 93:37). The powers of darkness surely disperse as we cleave unto light and truth.

*Aaron did expound unto him the scriptures from the creation of
Adam, laying the fall of man before him, and their carnal state
and also the plan of redemption, which was prepared
from the foundation of the world, through Christ,
for all whosoever would believe on his name.*

ALMA 22:13

It is given to only a few to have the kind of lasting
influence on human souls that the sons of Mosiah had
during their fourteen-year ministry. Why were they so
successful? Was it their attitude? Was it what they had
been taught by their parents? Was it the fear they felt
whenever they recalled the stunning visitation of an
angel, stopping them in their tracks? All of these may
have played a role in preparing them to make such a
significant contribution, but their effectiveness lay
largely in their love for the holy scriptures; when they
taught, they read or quoted or paraphrased holy writ.
They taught the great plan of redemption—the
Creation, the Fall, and the Atonement—and they did
so with power and authority from God. They read and
expounded upon the scriptures, the central message of
which was that redemption was in Christ.

*Since man had fallen he could not merit anything of himself; but
the sufferings and death of Christ atone for their sins, through
faith and repentance, and so forth; . . . and that the sting
of death should be swallowed up in the hopes of glory.*
ALMA 22:14

The word *merit* is used many times in the Book of
Mormon but never in reference to the merit of man.
The Book of Mormon is all about merit, but the doctrinal refrain of this testament of Christ is that
humankind, because of the Fall, cannot merit anything
of themselves. There are not enough meals and bread
and desserts to deliver, not enough home teaching and
visiting teaching visits to make, not enough meetings
to attend, and not enough prayers to offer for us to
save ourselves. True, we will stand before the bar of
God and be judged according to our works—but not
according to the *merits* of our works. Rather, good
works will stand as a manifestation of who and what
we have become through relying upon the merits and
mercy and grace of the Holy Messiah.

*O God, . . . if there is a God, and if thou art God, wilt thou
make thyself known unto me, and I will give away all my sins
to know thee, and that I may be raised from the dead,
and be saved at the last day.*

ALMA 22:18

Having been taught the plan of redemption and
what must be done to be saved, the father of King
Lamoni was moved to the core of his being. He did
the very thing that every genuine seeker after truth
must do to come unto Christ: He offered to surrender his will, his ways, and even his wealth. His desire
to have "this wicked spirit rooted out of [his] breast"—
that is, his desire to be born again—was strong enough
that he not only would forsake his kingdom gladly but,
more poignantly, forsake his sins to know the Lord
(Alma 22:15). Although he did not yet know for sure
that there is a God, his sweet petition to the heavens
bore witness of his sincerity and his compelling concern for his own soul. His remarkable conversion that
followed his prayer was evidence of the depth of his
contrition and his desire to serve that God he was
gradually coming to know.

As many as were brought to the knowledge of the truth, through the preaching of Ammon and his brethren, according to the spirit of revelation and of prophecy, and the power of God working miracles in them . . . and were converted unto the Lord, never did fall away.

ALMA 23:6

President Gordon B. Hinckley suggested three things to which every new convert to the Church is entitled: a friend, a responsibility or assignment, and to be "nourished by the good word of God" (Moroni 6:4; Conference Report, October 1997, 71). We know something about how the gospel was preached to the Lamanites by Ammon and the other sons of Mosiah—the way the missionaries lovingly interacted with the people, the doctrine they taught, and the way they were received by the members of the Church. There's something to be learned from this missionary account. Mormon teaches that those who were converted unto the Lord "never did fall away." Retention is always a product of true conversion—conversion of the members or the missionaries, and conversion of the new members. Both groups are built up, encouraged, strengthened, and retained by following the same principles.

It has been all that we could do, (as we were the most lost of all mankind) to repent of all our sins and the many murders which we have committed, . . . for it was all we could do to repent sufficiently before God that he would take away our stain.

ALMA 24:11

There is a very real sense in which "all we can do" (2 Nephi 25:23) is come before the Lord in reverent humility, confess our weakness, and plead for his forgiveness, for his mercy and grace. Life is repentance. Progression, improvement, growth, maturity, refinement are all forms of repentance. The truly god-fearing live in a state of constant repentance. It is not that we should live in fear or frustration or anxiety, but rather that we have desires for holiness and purity, longings to feel quiet confidence before God. Indeed, King Benjamin taught that those who regularly and consistently acknowledge the greatness of God and their own nothingness without him retain a remission of sins from day to day (Mosiah 4:11–12).

After a people have been once enlightened by the Spirit of God,
and have had great knowledge of things pertaining to righteousness,
and then have fallen away into sin and transgression, they become
more hardened, and thus their state becomes worse than
though they had never known these things.

ALMA 24:30

Since the beginning of time, some of the most hostile enemies of the kingdom of God and the prophets have been those who once embraced the faith. And yet, this very opposition is another testament of the truth. People leave various churches every year to accept the restored gospel, and they generally don't have bad feelings toward the churches they leave. Yet, as it has been said, when people leave the Church of Jesus Christ, they frequently cannot leave it alone. Many wear out their lives in bitter attacks against it. As Joseph Smith attested, there is no neutrality where the Church and kingdom of God are concerned (*Teachings, 67*). Once we embrace gospel truth, we are no longer on neutral ground: We have joined ourselves with light. If we later turn against what we once knew to be true, darkness will enter to fill its place and we become worse than before we embraced the truth. We must humbly and steadfastly hold on to the iron rod of truth.

Behold, my joy is full, yea, my heart is brim with joy, and I will rejoice in my God. Yea, I know that I am nothing; . . . therefore I will not boast of myself, but I will boast of my God, for in his strength I can do all things.

ALMA 26:11–12

Boasting about our accomplishments is a sure way to lose the Spirit, especially if the accomplishments are of a spiritual sort. With an eye single to the glory of God, we look to God and humbly acknowledge his hand in all things, as did Moses. "Man is nothing," Moses declared after viewing the expanses of eternity and learning of the majesty and power of God (Moses 1:10). Yet, with God's power, we can do all things in his name. The apostle Paul wrote, "I can do all things through Christ which strengtheneth me" (Philippians 4:13). This endowment of power is rightfully ours as His disciples, as long as we remain worthy. Man is nothing without divine intervention—but everything with it. If we are striving for righteousness and seeking the Spirit each day, we can do all that God wants us to do.

Behold, who can glory too much in the Lord? Yea, who can say too much of his great power, and of his mercy, and of his long-suffering towards the children of men? Behold, I say unto you, I cannot say the smallest part which I feel.

ALMA 26:16

Alma asked the people of Zarahemla: "If ye have experienced a change of heart, and if ye have felt to sing the song of redeeming love, I would ask, can ye feel so now?" (Alma 5:26). To sing the song of redeeming love is to rejoice in the goodness of the Father's plan; to exult in the Savior's atonement on our behalf; to feel the peaceful comfort that our course in life is pleasing to the Almighty; to have the assurance, set forth in scripture and witnessed by the Spirit, that life continues beyond the grave and that families can be forever; and to know with certainty that God has restored his everlasting gospel and conferred divine authority to modern apostles and prophets. If any people in all the world have reason to rejoice in the Lord, it is the Latter-day Saints. When we contemplate all that God has given to us and done for us, the spirit of thanksgiving and gratitude we should feel defies all expression.

We see that God is mindful of every people, whatsoever land they may be in; yea, he numbereth his people, and his bowels of mercy are over all the earth. Now this is my joy, and my great thanksgiving; yea, and I will give thanks unto my God forever. Amen.

ALMA 26:37

Our hearts overflow with rejoicing when we ponder the mercy of our God. Whether in this life or the next, the gospel will go to all people. All of his children can obtain the assurance of salvation through obedience to the laws and ordinances of the gospel. He wants us to become like him and share in his everlasting joy. Elder Boyd K. Packer taught: "No matter what citizenship or race, whether male or female, no matter what occupation, no matter your education, regardless of the generation in which one lives, life is a homeward journey for all of us, back to the presence of God in his celestial kingdom. Ordinances and covenants become our credentials for admission into His presence. To worthily receive them is the quest of a lifetime; to keep them thereafter is the challenge of mortality" (*Ensign,* May 1987, 24). Thanks be to God for his infinite love and his eternal plan of happiness.

Now the joy of Ammon was so great even that he was full; yea, he was swallowed up in the joy of his God, even to the exhausting of his strength. . . . Behold, this is joy which none receiveth save it be the truly penitent and humble seeker of happiness.

ALMA 27:17–18

Ammon and Alma had experienced the depths of true conversion together, and their friendship had been welded by the fire of the covenant. Upon meeting again and finding each other still faithful, they were filled with the Spirit of the Lord and rejoiced. So powerful were Ammon's feelings that he fell to the earth exhausted, without strength, as he had when he was overcome with the joy of the Spirit at Lamoni's conversion (Alma 19:12–14). In truth, we do experience joy in righteousness. Whenever the Spirit is with us, we feel joy, and we feel that joy most acutely in the manifestation that our sins have been remitted. Likewise, when the Spirit witnesses that our path is pleasing to God and approved by him or when we help others find the way to light and salvation, we feel great joy (Mosiah 4:3; D&C 18:13). Ultimately, exaltation consists in gaining a fulness of joy; it is to enter into the joy of the Lord (D&C 51:19).

Thus we see how great the inequality of man is because of sin and transgression, and the power of the devil, which comes by the cunning plans which he hath devised to ensnare the hearts of men.
ALMA 28:13

God's great leveling process by which "the poor shall be exalted, in that the rich are made low" (D&C 104:16) leads to unity. Zion is a society of the pure in heart, where "every man [seeks] the interest of his neighbor, and [does] all things with an eye single to the glory of God" (D&C 82:19). Division and inequality among people come through sin, through one desiring to have more than another and, in many cases, doing whatever it takes to obtain it. It has been said that wealth is a jealous master who will suffer no rivals and will not be served halfheartedly. Babylon is founded upon Satan's first article of faithlessness: A person can acquire anything in this world with money. Thus the great solution for world hunger and social inequality is not an increase in government programs but rather a turn to that Lord who is no respecter of persons.

*O that I were an angel, and could have the wish of mine heart,
that I might go forth and speak with the trump of God, with a
voice to shake the earth, and cry repentance unto every people!*

ALMA 29:1

Alma's sincere desire to lead people in the path of righteousness must have been like the desire of the angel who appeared to him and the four sons of Mosiah. That dramatic visitation prompted a mighty change in Alma and his friends. They humbly responded to the angelic ministration, and their lives were different ever after. As the angel called him to repentance, so Alma calls people of every nation to repent and come unto Christ every time the Book of Mormon is read. Millions have heard and will yet hear his voice, as the voice of an angel, resounding through the ages to touch hearts and bring souls to Christ. How sweet to imagine a world where all the inhabitants choose to live gospel standards! The peace, prosperity, and blessings that would follow would attest to the verity of the gospel plan. Such a condition is beyond the ability of our mortal minds to comprehend.

I am a man, and do sin in my wish; for I ought to be content with the things which the Lord hath allotted unto me.

ALMA 29:3

Wisely it has been said that in the Lord's service, it matters not *where* we serve but *how*. As members of the house of Israel, we have a vital mission to perform in saving members of our own family, ward, and community. Each of us is to be about our Father's business. Only as we do our part to build the kingdom can we experience the joy that comes from faithful service. A willing attitude toward service is a matter of agency. Only through the proper exercise of the divine gift of agency can we become like God. As with all of heaven's gifts, the power to exalt is matched by an equal power to condemn when misused. Agency is fruit plucked from the tree of life. In it are seeds which, if properly planted, nurtured, and pruned, will bear the fruits of salvation; but if allowed to grow wild, they will produce the gall of bitterness and eventual destruction. Agency is our glory or condemnation.

Behold, the Lord doth grant unto all nations, of their own nation and tongue, to teach his word, yea, in wisdom, all that he seeth fit that they should have; therefore we see that the Lord doth counsel in wisdom, according to that which is just and true.

ALMA 29:8

Our Heavenly Father knows the end from the beginning, and that exalted perspective enables him to govern his children and orchestrate the events of their lives in a way that would bring them the greatest happiness and fulfillment. He works according to a divine timetable, and he gives to his children that which they are ready to receive at a given time. In the spirit of both justice and mercy, the Omniscient One delivers truth to individuals and nations according to their capacity, their ability to perceive, appreciate, receive, and apply eternal truth. That God who will force no man to heaven will also not force anyone to acquire a truth or learn a lesson to which he or she is not open and receptive. As Isaiah taught, eventually the knowledge of God will cover the earth "as the waters cover the sea" (Isaiah 11:9), and the fulness of the everlasting gospel will be made available to every living soul, in this life or the next.

Many more such things did he say unto them, telling them that there could be no atonement made for the sins of men, but every man fared in this life according to the management of the creature; therefore . . . every man conquered according to his strength; and whatsoever a man did was no crime.

ALMA 30:17

Korihor contended that a Savior was not needed because it was impossible to sin. Because there is no absolute truth, he taught, there is no right or wrong. Like Nehor, Korihor argued that all success comes because of personal strength. He preached the self-improvement, motivational mantra of the day: the great god Me. In this way of thinking, man is the center of the universe: man has the power to solve his own problems and make himself happy—the power to do anything he sets his mind to. Humanism points toward man's genius, works, and accomplishments, but such consuming self-interest is profoundly antichristian, and though well received by the world, it is false, devilish, and destructive. It points us away from the Source that liberates us from this world's woes and brings happiness here and hereafter. It deflects our vision and our sense of dependence away from Christ and his divine grace. If we are truly to succeed, we must spend our lives in the service of God.

Ye also say that Christ shall come. But behold, I say that ye do not know that there shall be a Christ. And ye say also that he shall be slain for the sins of the world.
ALMA 30:26

As is often the case with antichrists, Korihor's worldview was extremely limited, and his vision of things as they really are was dim. He suffered from an ailment common to those who have attuned themselves meticulously to this temporal world: he overgeneralized from his own experience. Because he did not know, then surely no one else could know, either. Because he did not believe in prophecy, then surely no man could know of that which is to come. Because he had not received revelation, then surely no one could have the heavens opened unto them. Because he did not possess the testimony of Jesus, then surely there must be no Savior. It was unfortunate for Korihor that he had met his match—Alma was a seasoned veteran in the things of the Spirit. He had tasted and felt and come to know with a certain knowledge of that which is now and of that which is to come.

Thus we see the end of him who perverteth the ways of the Lord;
and thus we see that the devil will not support his children at
the last day, but doth speedily drag them down to hell.
ALMA 30:60

The example of Korihor is a stern warning to anyone who seeks to distort the principles of salvation and to lead others away in the process. One who chooses to do so has also chosen to join hands with the master of deceit, the father of all lies; he is in league with Lucifer. Unfortunately, the unwary eventually discover that Lucifer is entirely lacking in loyalty. From the time of our first estate in which he sought to amend or alter the plan of the Father to bring honor unto himself (Moses 4:1–4), his motives and his maneuvers have manifest his selfishness and megalomania. His actions are in stark contrast to the word and works of him who declared in the grand council: "Father, thy will be done, and the glory be thine forever" (Moses 4:2), the same One who, having trodden the winepress alone, was able to say before giving up the ghost, "Father, it is finished, thy will is done" (JST Matthew 27:54).

And now, as the preaching of the word had a great tendency to lead the people to do that which was just . . . therefore Alma thought it was expedient that they should try the virtue of the word of God.

ALMA 31:5

Often leaders resort to varied techniques of motivation. One may use incentives, another may buffet us with guilt, and still another may warn of impending doom if we are not faithful. On occasion each of these approaches can help to some extent to motivate others, but there is a tried and true method that only a few fully appreciate. It is simply this: Teach the gospel of Jesus Christ by the power of the Holy Ghost. Sometimes we almost seem to apologize for quoting a scripture when, in fact, Jesus and his angelic ministrants have frequently quoted scripture when they have appeared. Hearts are stirred and behavior is changed as we "try the virtue of the word of God," that is, when we have sufficient confidence in the scriptures and in the words of living prophets to preach the word boldly and without reservation. The Holy Ghost can then touch the hearts of others to join us in the work of the Lord.

Now, after the people had all offered up thanks after this manner,
they returned to their homes, never speaking of their God again
until they had assembled themselves together again to the holy
stand, to offer up thanks after their manner.

ALMA 31:23

In our dispensation the Lord has given the following commandment: "That thou mayest more fully
keep thyself unspotted from the world, thou shalt go
to the house of prayer and offer up thy sacraments,
upon my holy day; for verily this is a day appointed
unto you to rest from your labors, and to pay thy devo-
tions unto the Most High" (D&C 59:9–10). For
many, the Sabbath is the spiritual highlight of the
week, and to some extent, that is as it should be. We
take the sacrament of the Lord's Supper, listen to sermons and lessons, and interact with other Saints. But
the Sabbath is much more powerful when on the
other six days of the week we devote a portion of our
time to worshipping God and reflecting upon eternal
things. Thus the Savior added, "Nevertheless thy vows
shall be offered up in righteousness on all days and at
all times" (D&C 59:11).

Now as I said concerning faith—faith is not to have a perfect knowledge of things; therefore if ye have faith ye hope for things which are not seen, which are true.
ALMA 32:21

In Alma 32 we see Alma conducting, in effect, a Gospel Essentials class, speaking plainly and simply, knowing his listeners must be nurtured slowly. He defines faith from the viewpoint of mortality, not the vantage point of the eternities; otherwise, how would God, who has all knowledge, yet have the attribute of faith? (Hebrews 11:3). In our present world, faith assures us of the existence of the unseen. Faith is a divine process built upon knowledge and understanding of eternal verities as well as upon personal righteousness. We may possess a slight amount of faith—having but little understanding of the gospel, and living but a portion of the gospel law—or we may possess the kind of faith that moves mountains (Ether 12:30). Faith is not positive thinking. Faith is power, knowledge, conviction, and action. Faith leads us to believe in the Lord and accept the words of his anointed servants. Faith in Jesus Christ leads to life everlasting.

September

The preaching of the word had a
great tendency to lead the people to
do that which was just—yea, it
had had more powerful effect upon
the minds of the people than the
sword, or anything else.

Alma 31:5

*Awake and arouse your faculties, even to an experiment upon my
words, and exercise a particle of faith, yea, even if ye can no more
than desire to believe, let this desire work in you, even until ye
believe in a manner that ye can give place for a portion of my words.*
ALMA 32:27

The quest for truth is essentially an experiment
upon the words of Christ. That is the most vital
experiment we ever undertake, because its rewards are
eternal. When we waken as if from a deep sleep and
set aside distractions, we yearn to know the things of
eternity. The initial motivator is a simple desire, a
hunger to know. We study, ponder, and pray. We seek
out others who have experimented upon the word of
God, others who have gained testimonies and can
guide us. We live in righteous accord with the truth
growing inside our hearts. The particle of faith takes
root and begins to blossom and grow. Our faith
expands along with our knowledge. Little by little, line
upon line, our confidence in the Lord begins to wax
strong. Our testimonies which were once so tiny, now,
like the mighty oak, stand steadfast and immovable.
All this from a diminutive desire, a fragment of faith,
an honest heart, and real intent.

*It is because of thy Son that thou hast been thus merciful unto me,
therefore I will cry unto thee in all mine afflictions, for in
thee is my joy; for thou hast turned thy judgments
away from me, because of thy Son.*

ALMA 33:11

The teachings of Zenos and Zenock, two prophets
whose writings were on the brass plates, spoke eloquently
to Alma and to us concerning how and where to offer up
petitions to God. Zenos reminded us that there is purpose for our suffering in this life, purposes often veiled
from our present understanding. Suffering makes us
more empathetic towards those about us who struggle,
more willing to lift and lighten their burdens. In addition,
suffering can make saints out of sinners, for it initiates us
into the fellowship of Christ's suffering. Often it is in our
extremity that we acknowledge our weakness, confess his
greatness, and thereby become acquainted with God. The
Man of Sorrows, the Suffering Servant, descended below
all things that he might comprehend all things (D&C
88:6). Similarly, as we are called upon to be stretched and
broken and torn by the ironies of this existence, our
hearts are softened and we find our souls more attuned
to the voice of heaven.

*It is expedient that there should be a great and last sacrifice.
And behold, this is the whole meaning of the law, every whit
pointing to that great and last sacrifice; and that great and last
sacrifice will be the Son of God, yea, infinite and eternal.*
ALMA 34:10, 14

A universal fall required a universal atonement. The atonement of Jesus Christ is infinite in that it is timeless: Adam and Eve and their children were taught to repent and call upon God because of an atonement that would be made some four thousand years later (Alma 39:17–19; Moses 5:5–8). The Atonement is infinite in that it engages and overcomes the most universal of all eternal roadblocks: physical and spiritual death (2 Nephi 9:7). The Atonement is infinite in that it stretches well beyond this world, for Jesus is the Creator and Redeemer of worlds without number. What he creates, he redeems (D&C 76:24; Moses 1:32, 35). Finally, the Atonement is infinite and eternal in that Jesus is an infinite and eternal being (Alma 34:14), the only one capable of facing the assaults of Gethsemane, the agony of the cross, and death itself, emerging victorious from them all.

Now is the time and the day of your salvation; and therefore, if ye will repent and harden not your hearts, immediately shall the great plan of redemption be brought about unto you. For behold, this life is the time for men to prepare to meet God.

ALMA 34:31–32

In a sense, every day is a day of decision. We must decide whether we will continue faithful, remain open to spiritual promptings, and keep our covenants. We must decide whether we will continue to pause on our present spiritual plateau or choose instead to fight the inertia and climb higher. Every thought, every feeling, every action contributes to who we are and what we are becoming, and thus either adds or detracts from the eventual realization of our salvation. Thus today is "the time for men to prepare to meet God." There is nothing we can do about the past, except to repent, and the future doesn't belong to us yet. We have only now. If we are striving to keep the commandments and cultivate the spirit of revelation, then it could be said of us, as it was said of former-day Saints, that "now is our salvation nearer than when we believed" (Romans 13:11).

I beseech of you that ye do not procrastinate the day of your repentance until the end; for after this day of life, . . . then cometh the night of darkness wherein there can be no labor performed.

ALMA 34:33

We are setting the pattern today for where we will be and what we will do tomorrow. It has wisely been said that procrastination is the thief of eternal life, for it robs us of future opportunities and leads us to forfeit available blessings. The Prophet Joseph Smith issued a "warning to all not to procrastinate repentance, or wait till a death-bed, for it is the will of God that man should repent and serve Him in health, and in the strength and power of his mind, in order to secure His blessing and not wait until he is called to die" (*Teachings,* 197). Further, putting off our repentance until a future day places us in a habitual course, thus making change that much more difficult. We will leave this earth life with a certain disposition: either an inclination to resist the truth or a propensity to embrace it. Now is the time to decide which way we will go.

He said unto me: If thou wilt of thyself be destroyed,
seek no more to destroy the church of God.

ALMA 36:9

While moral agency is foundational to the very plan of salvation—a vital principle over which the war in heaven was fought and over which battles continue to rage today—there are limits beyond which the God of heaven will not allow humankind to halt the progress of the work of salvation. Saul of Tarsus was busily engaged in persecuting the Christians when the resurrected Jesus appeared and brought about a remarkable transformation in the heart of that zealous Pharisee (Acts 9:22, 26). Alma and the sons of Mosiah were likewise engaged in destroying the church of God when an angel caused Alma and his friends to consider their ways. The angel said to Alma, in essence, if you want to destroy yourself, then go right ahead, but you will no longer be allowed to destroy the church of God. The destiny of the Lord's kingdom is set. What is undecided is where each of us will stand in regard to that ongoing kingdom.

Behold, I remembered also to have heard my father prophesy unto the people concerning the coming of one Jesus Christ, a Son of God, to atone for the sins of the world. . . . I cried within my heart: O Jesus, thou Son of God, have mercy on me.

ALMA 36:17–18

When we feel like we can't go on, the Savior offers sweet assurance, "I am come that they might have life, and that they might have it more abundantly" (John 10:10). When we feel alone and afraid, he beckons, "Come unto me, all ye that labour and are heavy laden, and I will give you rest" (Matthew 11:28). When all seems dark and dreary, he lifts us with his radiant life. This is the Christ who calmed the raging wind and water of Galilee, "Peace, be still" (Mark 4:39). And though his miracles were many, the greatest miracle of all is his divine grace and bounteous mercy. This is our Redeemer, who grants us newness of life according to our faith and repentance, who sheds upon us his loving kindness, who brings us peace here and salvation hereafter.

> *Nor voice can sing, nor heart can frame,*
> *Nor can the mem'ry find*
> *A sweeter sound than thy blest name,*
> *O Savior of mankind!*
>
> (Hymns, no. 141)

I say unto you, my son, that there could be nothing so exquisite and so bitter as were my pains. Yea, and again I say unto you, my son, that on the other hand, there can be nothing so exquisite and sweet as was my joy.

ALMA 36:21

The Spirit brings joy and light; sin and evil invite misery and darkness. True repentance is always attended by a spirit of rejoicing (Mosiah 4:3); even the angels in heaven rejoice over us when we repent (D&C 62:3). The paradox of godly sorrow is that out of the depths of repentance, the pain and anguish of a sorrowful soul, is born the most exquisite joy. Without the suffering associated with true repentance, we cannot experience this consummate joy. Sincere repentance, which centers on faith in Christ and his atoning sacrifice, requires sufficient suffering on our part until we are refined enough to become one in mind and soul with the Savior. The blessings of salvation, though freely given, have been bought with an infinite price. In all things we must unite our best effort with him who sacrificed all. Great joy comes to those who are born of God, those who are filled with the Holy Ghost, those who know the sweet peace of forgiveness (Alma 36:23–26).

*I have been supported under trials and troubles of every kind, . . .
yea, God has delivered me from prison, and from bonds, and from
death. . . . And I know that he will raise me up at the last day,
to dwell with him in glory; yea, and I will praise him forever.*
ALMA 36:27–28

Alma, seasoned by the Spirit and refined by life's trials, reflected upon his mortal journey with thanksgiving. His heart overflowed with praise and gratitude to God, who has taught him, upheld him, and redeemed him from sin and death. His confidence waxed strong in the Lord as he testified of heaven's bountiful blessings and merciful providence. Alma understood well the principles of faith, repentance, and forgiveness. This disciple of Jesus was a mighty man of God who had become a new creature in Christ and spent his days striving to bring others into the family of Christ. Through his many crucibles, he became an inspiration that we can never forget. His life was a testament to God's mercy, to what he himself called "the great plan of happiness" (Alma 42:8), to the entire message of redeeming love exemplified by the Savior. Alma's spiritual maturity is evident as his whole heart was turned toward trusting God and praising his name.

Now ye may suppose that this is foolishness in me; but behold I say unto you, that by small and simple things are great things brought to pass; and small means in many instances doth confound the wise.
ALMA 37:6

Little things matter. Those who inherit the highest degree of the celestial kingdom will be those who become partakers of the divine nature through regular attention to small things. Walking to Missouri, offering to give one's life for the faith, or baptizing a nation may not be the actions that will bring about the greatest good; it is, rather, the little things—the smile, the gentle touch, the selfless gesture, the unanticipated compliment, the quiet response to an inner prompting to serve—that will bring about great good. "Wherefore, be not weary in well-doing, for ye are laying the foundation of a great work. And out of small things proceedeth that which is great. Behold, the Lord requireth the heart and a willing mind; and the willing and obedient shall eat the good of the land of Zion in these last days" (D&C 64:33–34). Zion is established "in process of time" (Moses 7:21), and the march to that holy city begins with a single step.

*Preach unto them repentance, and faith on the Lord Jesus Christ;
teach them to humble themselves and to be meek and lowly in
heart; teach them to withstand every temptation of the devil,
with their faith on the Lord Jesus Christ.*

ALMA 37:33

We are able to encounter and overcome evil but not simply through greater and greater displays of willpower and grit, as important as such things are. We become pure in heart not just because we have developed a more disciplined lifestyle, though such is basic to Christian discipleship. The inhabitants of the celestial world are they "who overcome by faith" (D&C 76:53), those whose reliance upon the person and powers of Jesus Christ are certain and sure. The Master becomes not only our model and our exemplar but also our source of strength and our reason to carry on. Thanks be to God that the Messiah has come to earth, "even Jesus Christ, your advocate, who knoweth the weakness of man and how to succor them who are tempted" (D&C 62:1).

*O, remember, my son, and learn wisdom in thy youth; yea, learn
in thy youth to keep the commandments of God.*

ALMA 37:35

Alma knew firsthand the anguish of soul that comes
to those who choose wickedness, who reject the righteous counsel of prophets and parents. For three days
he had been racked with the pains of a damned soul,
experiencing inexpressible horror at the thought of
meeting his Maker, feeling encircled about with the
everlasting chains of death (Alma 37:6–28). Jesus rescued him from the gall of bitterness and set him on
the path of mighty change. Alma earnestly counseled
his sons to learn from the mistakes of his own early
life. Turn to Christ and his atonement now, hate sin
and iniquity, be meek and lowly in heart, do good
works. The wisest course to follow—especially when
followed from one's youth—is to keep the commandments of God and experience true joy and happiness.

Cry unto God for all thy support; yea, let all thy doings be unto the Lord, and whithersoever thou goest let it be in the Lord; yea, let all thy thoughts be directed unto the Lord; . . . and if ye do these things, ye shall be lifted up at the last day.

ALMA 37:36–37

The Lord will surely guide and bless us if we turn to him with full purpose of heart. All through the day, we can think, *What would I do if the Savior stood beside me?* or *What would thou have me do?* With a prayer in our heart all day long, our personal prayers—both morning and night—take on a new dimension. As we practice listening to the whisperings of the Spirit, we become more familiar with the Lord and his ways and can better align our petitions with his will. If we are humble enough to be to be guided by Christ's sacred influence, the Spirit will show us all things that we should do (2 Nephi 32:3, 5). The wisdom of ages past is of vital importance in our day: "Trust in the Lord will all thine heart; and lean not unto thine own understanding. In all thy ways acknowledge him, and he shall direct thy paths" (Proverbs 3:5–6).

See that ye take care of these sacred things, yea,
see that ye look to God and live.
ALMA 37:47

We must take special care to safeguard sacred things: the doctrines and principles of everlasting life, our covenants and ordinances, our faithfulness to the Lord and adoration of him. These must be vigilantly watched over and protected. We do not speak of holy things in a light-minded way, nor do we treat the things of eternity casually. That doesn't mean we are somber and serious at all times. Those who have internalized real spirituality have a smile on their face, a spring in their step, and tend to be light-hearted as they look on the positive side of things—even amidst difficulties and challenges. President Gordon B. Hinckley has counseled us, "Let us live the gospel. Let it shine in our lives. Let it shine in our faces. Let it come through our actions. Live the gospel. Look to God and live" (*Stand a Little Taller*, 32). The pathway always seems brighter when we truly look heavenward and live with integrity and devotion to God.

*Use boldness, but not overbearance; and also see that ye bridle
all your passions, that ye may be filled with love;
see that ye refrain from idleness.*

ALMA 38:12

It is unfortunate that the romantic concept of love
has dominated western civilization for centuries. This
false view holds that love is some sort of scintillating
feeling that suddenly sweeps into a person's life like
the blowing wind, settles for a season, and may leave
as unexpectedly as it came. It is defined by the emotional fireworks between two persons who are said to
love each other. True love certainly has emotional
components, but it is much, much more than a feeling. It is a commitment, a vow, a conscious determination to see to the happiness and well-being of the
beloved. It is far deeper than physical attraction and
physical intimacy, far more profound than that which
is portrayed on the movie screens and television sit-
coms. It is experienced most poignantly by the righteous, who have bridled their passions and harnessed
their ego, who have given themselves to the Lord and
devoted themselves to others.

*Know ye not, my son, that these things are an abomination in the
sight of the Lord; yea, most abominable above all sins save it be
the shedding of innocent blood or denying the Holy Ghost?*
ALMA 39:5

God is in charge of all matters pertaining to life and
death. He is very concerned about how mortals leave
this second estate and go into the postmortal spirit
world. He is equally concerned about how and under
what circumstances a premortal spirit enters the second estate. And so, as Alma taught, unauthorized sexual experience is an abomination in the sight of him
who gave us life. Such sin is ranked in seriousness only
behind the sin against the Holy Ghost and murder.
But though the sin against the Holy Ghost is unpar-
donable and the taking of human life unforgivable,
sexual immorality is forgivable, though not easy. One
cannot tamper with the fountains of life without
offending the Spirit and alienating oneself from the
things of righteousness.

*Behold, it has been made known unto me by an angel, that the
spirits of all men, as soon as they are departed from this mortal
body, yea, the spirits of all men, whether they be good or evil,
are taken home to that God who gave them life.*
ALMA 40:11

The Book of Mormon bears witness that life does
not end when one goes through the experience of
physical death. It is the common lot of all who come
into this life. Everyone who is born must, sooner or
later, die. We are born as helpless infants, and we
depart helpless in the face of death. In the purest
sense, however, there is no death, and there are no
dead. When living things die, they do not cease to
be—they merely cease to be in this world. Life goes on.
Death is a transition, a change in assignment, a trans-
fer to another realm. When we die, the spirit continues to see and act and feel and associate; it is only the
physical body that becomes inactive and lifeless for a
season. And so our term *death* describes things from
our limited mortal perspective. From an eternal perspective, there is only life.

The soul shall be restored to the body, and the body to the soul;
yea, and every limb and joint shall be restored to its body; yea,
even a hair of the head shall not be lost; but all things shall be
restored to their proper and perfect frame.

ALMA 40:23

All who have taken a physical body will be resurrected. Through the mercy of the Savior, every person who has breathed the breath of life will rise from the dead. The spirit and the body will be reunited, inseparably joined, never again to be divided (Alma 11:43; 40:23; D&C 138:17). The apostle Paul wrote: "If in this life only we have hope in Christ, we are of all men most miserable. But now is Christ risen from the dead, and become the firstfruits of them that slept. For since by man came death, by man came also the resurrection of the dead. For as in Adam all die, even so in Christ shall all be made alive" (1 Corinthians 15:19–22; compare Isaiah 25:8). Ours is a living faith in Christ. Our identities shall continue after death, and the reunion with departed loved ones will contribute to what the scriptures call "a fulness of joy" (D&C 93:33).

*It is requisite with the justice of God that men should be judged
according to their works; and if their works were good in this life,
and the desires of their hearts were good, that they should also,
at the last day, be restored unto that which is good.*

ALMA 41:3

How perfect the wisdom and mercy of our God!
Both heart and hand will be weighed in the balance on
Judgment Day. This divine combination reveals our
true character better than either works or desires
alone. We will each account for what we did in the circumstances that were ours, as well as for what we
would have done if we had been allowed control over
those circumstances. There will be those who would
have done more if they could and those who could
have done more than they did. The Lord knows what
went into shaping who we really are; he also knows our
capabilities and our potential. How reassuring that he
who knows all things knows each of us individually. He
sees our works; he knows our hearts. Thanks be to
God that we will be judged not alone for our deeds but
also according to the desires of our hearts (D&C
137:9).

Behold, I say unto you, wickedness never was happiness.
ALMA 41:10

The central message of holy writ, that wickedness cannot produce happiness, is the purpose for all the laws and ordinances our Father has given us. He wants us to be happy and have eternal life. This gift can be ours only if we prepare ourselves for it, however. Those consumed by worldly ways may prosper by the world's standards for a season, but they will never know true happiness. They will not know the joy that comes from hearkening to the light within that bids us to do good (3 Nephi 27:11). They will not know the "peace of God, which passeth all understanding" and which comes to those who love the Lord and seek to do his will (Philippians 4:7). The dead-end detours of momentary pleasure and carnal gratification cannot satisfy the infinite longing of the soul for the strait and narrow path of truth, integrity, and righteousness. Lasting joy and heartfelt peace come only to those who follow the Savior and his prophets and keep the commandments.

See that you are merciful unto your brethren; deal justly, judge righteously, and do good continually; and if ye do all these things . . . ye shall have good rewarded unto you again. For that which ye do send out shall return unto you.

ALMA 41:14–15

The ultimate Golden Rule is that we should treat others the way we want our Eternal Judge to treat us. If we are merciful, just, and righteous, we shall have mercy and justice rewarded unto us. That is, we will be saved in the kingdom of God (Matthew 10:41). Many times we think of justice as that which is rightfully due the wicked. But justice also comes to the faithful (2 Nephi 9:46). True disciples of the Lord seek to become even as he is: overflowing in mercy, walking with fairness and integrity, making righteous judgments, always abounding in good works. "What doth the Lord require of thee, but to do justly, and to love mercy, and to walk humbly with thy God?" (Micah 6:8). That which we send out will come back to us—whether blessing or punishment. May we walk in mercy and goodness and receive the reward of righteousness.

There is a law given, and a punishment affixed, and a repentance granted; which repentance, mercy claimeth; otherwise, justice claimeth the creature and executeth the law, and the law inflicteth the punishment; if not so, the works of justice would be destroyed, and God would cease to be God.

ALMA 42:22

Some have taken Alma 42:22 to mean that it is possible for God to cease to be God, that if he should, by some bizarre means, fail to function in perfectness, he would be unseated and removed from his place of preeminence. Such ideas are to some quite stimulating. They are, nonetheless, erroneous and misleading. God will not and cannot cease to be God. His title, his status, and his exalted position are forever fixed and immutable. Exalted beings simply do not apostatize. They do not slip. It is contrary to their divine nature to lie or cheat or be partial. God does not depend on others for his Godhood, nor can he be impeached. The Saints of God need not spend a particle of a second worrying and fretting about the Almighty falling from grace. To do so is to err in doctrine and to fall short of that dynamic faith that leads to life and salvation.

Now, my son, I desire that ye should let these things trouble you no more, and only let your sins trouble you, with that trouble which shall bring you down unto repentance.

ALMA 42:29

If we are to remain on the strait and narrow path, we must understand a proper remorse of conscience. We must distinguish between the devil's dissonance (which is demoralizing and counterproductive) and divine discontent (which is a godly invitation for gradual and constant improvement). True Saints pray to know that they are in good standing with the Lord. They ask the Father to help them desire righteousness and resist temptation. They know that they are not to beat themselves up endlessly over past misdeeds. But no one seeking salvation would want to feel any less guilt than is required for complete forgiveness. "Now I rejoice," Paul wrote, "not that ye were made sorry, but that ye sorrowed to repentance." And then the apostle added: "For godly sorrow worketh repentance to salvation," while "the sorrow of the world worketh death" (2 Corinthians 7:9–10). We are to remember our past sins enough to stay far away from them and then faithfully go forward.

The design of the Nephites was to support their lands, and their houses, and their wives, and their children, that they might preserve them from the hands of their enemies; and also that they might preserve . . . their liberty, that they might worship God according to their desires.

ALMA 43:9

Only the perverse and foolish enjoy war. No sane human being relishes the thought of placing his own life in jeopardy or of taking the life of another in military action. Thus the message given over and over in the Book of Mormon is that we enter war only as a defensive measure and only as it is necessary to preserve the sacred gift of moral agency when it is under attack by others (Alma 43:45–47). The wisest among us, even those who are not members of the household of faith, plead for divine direction and the support and blessings of heaven whenever circumstances require us to enter a war. The Saints have been instructed to "first lift a standard of peace" and then pray that the differences may be resolved, for the Savior has declared that if we trust in him, "I, the Lord, [will] fight their battles" (D&C 98:34, 37).

Thus we see how quick the children of men do forget the Lord their God, yea, how quick to do iniquity, and to be led away by the evil one. Yea, and we also see the great wickedness one very wicked man can cause to take place among the children of men.

ALMA 46:8–9

Amalickiah was a strong man of cunning devices who, more than anything else, wanted to reign as king and totalitarian monarch over the people. He used flattering words and appealed to those who shared his pride and desire for power, but he truly cared only about himself. Why do we so easily forget the Lord and heed the words of such pundits? We must maintain our spiritual posture to make righteous judgments, to beware of false prophets whose only wish is to attract supporters and thereby gain power. Committed followers of the Savior bring others to him, give him all glory and honor, and continually point others toward earth's true joys and heaven's eternal rewards. They fulfill their stewardship responsibilities with integrity and humility, always looking to the Lord for strength and wisdom. One person can make a tremendous difference for good or for evil. We can be one who makes a positive difference and brings others to Christ.

Yea, verily, verily I say unto you, if all men had been, and were, and ever would be, like unto Moroni, behold, the very powers of hell would have been shaken forever; yea, the devil would never have power over the hearts of the children of men.

ALMA 48:17

No greater tribute could be paid to a man than that which Mormon paid to Captain Moroni. Moroni did not like war. He abhorred the shedding of blood. He was a man of prophetic stature, one who enjoyed the spirit of prophecy and revelation, one who was close to that Lord he served. These qualities were far more critical elements of his powerful leadership than any policy or program or ingenious strategy that may have been put into effect by Moroni during the years of war. Indeed, if there were more Moronis, there would be many fewer wars, Satan's progress would be halted, and the people of planet Earth would be made more ready to receive their Heavenly King.

*They were exceedingly valiant for courage, and also for strength
and activity; but behold, this was not all—they were men who
were true at all times in whatsoever thing they were entrusted. . . .
they had been taught to keep the commandments of
God and to walk uprightly before him.*

ALMA 53:20–21

The story of Helaman's two thousand stripling warriors is an account of a significant historical moment in Nephite history. It stands as a symbol of the courage, fearlessness, and goodness that characterize individuals and nations who are "true at all times in whatsoever thing they [are] entrusted." It was not just that the stripling warriors were men of faith because they knew the truths of the gospel (for, as Helaman observed, they had been taught by their mothers not to doubt; Alma 56:47–48). More important, they were true. Knowing the truth is one thing; living the truth, embodying the truth, and being true is something else again. As Jesus would declare in another hemisphere almost a century later, every person that does evil hates the light, "but he that doeth truth cometh to the light" (John 3:21).

Because of the exceedingly great length of the war between the
Nephites and the Lamanites many had become hardened, . . .
and many were softened because of their afflictions,
insomuch that they did humble themselves before God,
even in the depth of humility.

ALMA 62:41

It is inevitable that challenges and obstacles and traumas will come into our lives; they are the stuff of which mortality is made. Hard times come to all of us sooner or later. The issue, then, is not so much whether such things will come but when and, more significantly, how we will respond to them. The question so often asked by the weary or the downtrodden, Why is this happening to me? is seldom helpful, for the answer is simple: This is what mortality is all about. More profitable questions that might be asked during times of trial are, What can I learn from this experience? How would the Lord have me respond? What action and attitude would bring me the greatest insight? How can I draw lessons from these difficult times that may one day bless the lives of others? Those who take such an approach find their hearts softened, their trust in the Lord strengthened, and their burdens lighter.

The Lord is merciful unto all who will, in the sincerity of their hearts, call upon his holy name. Yea, thus we see that the gate of heaven is open unto all, even to those who will believe on the name of Jesus Christ, who is the Son of God.

HELAMAN 3:27–28

The church of God, during this period in the record, had spiritually prospered with tens of thousands of converts. Peace and joy and outpourings of blessings were the way of life for the faithful Saints (Helaman 3:24–28). The Lord would like to bless all people in this way. He is mindful of everyone who calls upon his holy name and is merciful to them. God is no "respecter of persons" (Acts 10:34). Abundant blessings are available to all who are willing to be transformed by gospel teachings (2 Nephi 26:33). But though heaven's gate is surely open to all, they who enter therein must be willing to humble themselves in keeping the commandments. They exercise faith, repent, and give away their sins. They enter the waters of baptism and receive the Holy Ghost. Thereafter, they remain true and faithful to covenants, diligently keep the commandments, serve others, and grow in gospel light. This is the pathway to eternal life.

Pride . . . began to enter into the church—not into the church of God, but into the hearts of the people who professed to belong to the church of God—And they were lifted up in pride, even to the persecution of many of their brethren.

HELAMAN 3:33–34

Once again, pride had entered the hearts of many members of the Nephite Church. Feeling self-important, they persecuted the more humble Saints. Where there is pride, there is hostility toward others, both in and out of the Church. Pride always stems from the same source: enmity, whether it is looking down on others with condescension and arrogance or looking up at others in envy and covetousness. President Gordon B. Hinckley has said: "We can be more tolerant, more neighborly, more friendly, more of an example than we have been in the past. Let us teach our children to treat others with friendship, respect, love, and admiration. That will yield a far better result than will an attitude of egotism and arrogance" (*Ensign,* May 2000, 87). Those who know better, those who have been enlightened and prospered by gospel truth, have an increased accountability (D&C 82:3). True followers of Christ strive for relationships of peace and unity.

OCTOBER

*I came into the world to do the
will of my Father, because my
Father sent me. . . . As I have been
lifted up by men even so should
men be lifted up by the Father, to
stand before me, to be judged of
their works.*

3 NEPHI 27:13–14

They did fast and pray oft, and did wax stronger and stronger in
their humility, and firmer and firmer in the faith of Christ, unto
the filling their souls with joy and consolation, yea, even to the
purifying and the sanctification of their hearts.

HELAMAN 3:35

Oftentimes when we feel buffeted by the world, our hearts turn more to heaven. Fasting and praying help to increase our faith and fill our souls with joy and consolation. Even amidst affliction, firm faith in Christ brings "the peaceable things of the kingdom" (D&C 36:2; 42:61). Peace and joy have been promised to those who faithfully seek the Savior (John 14:27). Thus, to give our hearts to God is humbly but diligently to inquire his mind and will, to meekly follow the impressions of the Spirit, and to keep our eyes single to the glory of God. Sanctification comes by the power of the Holy Ghost only to those who "overcome by faith" (D&C 76:53). In other words, sanctification comes through yielding our hearts to Christ.

*Because of this their great wickedness, and their boastings in
their own strength, they were left in their own strength;
therefore they did not prosper, but were afflicted and smitten,
and driven before the Lamanites, until they had lost
possession of almost all their lands.*

HELAMAN 4:13

One of the values of reading and rereading the
Book of Mormon is the constant reemergence of
invaluable precepts, precepts that when abided by will
bring us closer to God (Smith, *Teachings,* 194.) Those
who refuse to acknowledge the omnipotence and
omniscience of God and thus refuse to incorporate his
consummate power fight their battles and engage
their Goliaths on their own. They are left to themselves, to their own futile philosophies, and their own
erroneous efforts. On the other hand, those who
acknowledge their weakness, turn to the Lord God for
strength, and plead for his divine enabling power gain
a perspective and a power well beyond their own finite
resources. As the apostle Paul wrote, "For my strength
is made perfect in weakness . . . for when I am weak,
then am I strong" (2 Corinthians 12:9–10).

I have given unto you the names of our first parents who came out of the land of Jerusalem; and this I have done that when you remember your names ye may remember them; and when ye remember them ye may remember their works . . . that they were good.

HELAMAN 5:6

Nephi and Lehi were named after the first prophets recorded in the Book of Mormon. Their father, Helaman, named them after these righteous men, some six hundred years later, in the hope that they would remember the faithfulness of their namesakes. Many parents today have the same intent. Often parents name a son or daughter for an ancestor, a person they admire, a friend who made a difference. This generational continuity links the past, present, and future in a chain of treasured memories, righteous remembrances, and inspiring models. Of course, the most important name for each person is the immutable imprint that we are beloved sons and daughters of heavenly parents, each with a divine nature and destiny (Proclamation on the Family). As God's children, we are called by his name.

*Now, my sons, remember, remember that it is upon the rock
of our Redeemer, who is Christ, the Son of God, that ye must
build your foundation; that when the devil shall send forth
his mighty winds, . . . it shall have no power over you.*
HELAMAN 5:12

The rock of our Redeemer is the sure foundation in
life, the one that will never falter or fail. When all else
falls apart, when sore troubles come upon us, when we
feel buffeted by the burdens and difficulties of life, our
Savior is there sustaining us in our trials, comforting
us in our heartaches, and strengthening us in our weak
moments. It is to him we must look with adoration
and devotion. It is upon his atonement and truth that
salvation is built. The many things that we can build
our foundation upon—intelligence, possessions, status, appearance, ad infinitum—will disappoint and
fade away with time. But the Savior—steady, strong,
solid—will ever be with us if we enter into his new and
everlasting gospel covenant and remain faithful.
Christ, our sure foundation, is the way to happiness
and peace in this world and in the world to come.

That same being who put it into the heart of Gadianton to still
carry on the work of darkness . . . has brought it forth from
the beginning of man even down to this time. And behold,
it is he who is the author of all sin. . . . he had got
great hold upon the hearts of the Nephites.

HELAMAN 6:29–31

Evil oaths and secret covenants always come from the father of lies, the adversary of righteousness. His followers work in darkness; their desire is gain, power, self-aggrandizement. Their weapon of choice is usually pride. These evildoers want to get hold of our hearts, turn us away from righteousness, and trample underfoot the commandments of God. It has ever been thus. From the premortal council in heaven, to the Garden of Eden, to Gadianton's robbers and murderers, the appeal is the same: get people to be selfish, consume them with self-interest, sneak a lie into a bouquet of truths, teach them that life is a competition, and convince them to live for the day with no thought of tomorrow (2 Nephi 28:7–8). This myopic, haughty approach to life will inevitably lead to contention and enmity—both of which destroy homes and hearts and turn us away from God's path. But if we follow the Light of the World, he will lift us from darkness into light.

Oh, that I could have had my days in the days when my father Nephi first came out of the land of Jerusalem, . . . then would my soul have had joy in the righteousness of my brethren.
HELAMAN 7:7–8

Nephi and his family knew much conflict and wickedness. Jacob wrote about their time, "We being a lonesome and a solemn people, wanderers, cast out from Jerusalem, born in tribulation, in a wilderness, and hated of our brethren, which caused wars and contentions; wherefore, we did mourn out our days" (Jacob 7:26). In the midst of turmoil, we may long for the days of yore. We may forget the less desirable elements of the past and remember only the happy moments and cherished experiences—which is not all bad. But in doing so we overlook an important lesson. Those who went before us also had their challenges. Life was never intended to be easy. A hundred years from now people may look back and wish they had lived in the first part of the twenty-first century. The better approach is to remember the past with gratitude, live with joy in the present, and have great hope for the future.

How could you have forgotten your God in the very day that he has delivered you? But behold, it is to get gain, to be praised of men, yea, and that ye might get gold and silver.

HELAMAN 7:20–21

The curse of riches is a common theme in the Book of Mormon. Prophet after prophet urges an eternal perspective where we turn to everlasting things and turn away from the allures of the world. The enticements of Babylon, the arm of flesh, will always disappoint us in the long run. President Heber J. Grant said: "Next to the committing of sin there is no more fruitful cause of apostasy among the Latter-day Saints than when we put our trust in the arm of flesh. I firmly believe that no man who honestly bows down every day of his life and supplicates God in sincerity for the light of His Holy Spirit to guide him will ever become proud and haughty. On the contrary, his heart will become filled with meekness, humility, and child-like simplicity" (*Gospel Standards,* 31). If we always remember from whence our blessings come and keep the Lord foremost in our lives, we'll avoid many of the traps that prosperity can set for us.

*As he lifted up the brazen serpent in the wilderness, even so shall
he be lifted up who should come. And as many as should look upon
that serpent should live, even so as many as should look upon the
Son of God with faith, having a contrite spirit, might live.*

HELAMAN 8:14–15

When the Savior visited the New World, he
announced that the Mosaic law was fulfilled in him.
He said, "Behold, I am the law, and the light. Look
unto me, and endure to the end, and ye shall live; for
unto him that endureth to the end will I give eternal
life" (3 Nephi 15:9). The ancient law was to direct our
attention to the Lawgiver. The brazen serpent was to
foreshadow our looking to the everlasting life found
in Christ, who was lifted upon the cross of Calvary.
Then as now, peace and joy are found by looking to
the Savior with full purpose of heart. He is the Light
of the World, our "bright and morning star"
(Revelation 22:16), our exemplar and ideal. As we
learn of him and follow him, we move along the path
to eternal life.

Behold, ye have rejected the truth, and rebelled against your holy God; and even at this time, instead of laying up for yourselves treasures in heaven, . . . where nothing can come which is unclean, ye are heaping up for yourselves wrath against the day of judgment.

HELAMAN 8:25

Because each of us is less than perfect, we all need the Lord's amazing grace. The day of judgment will be great to those who hold fast to the truth and stand firm in the faith. "All persons will be judged according to the deeds done in the flesh; as their works have been here in mortality, so shall their rewards be in immortality," wrote Elder Bruce R. McConkie. "This means they will be judged for their beliefs, or in other words for their thoughts, their words, and their acts" (*New Witness*, 25). The Savior said, "Out of the abundance of the heart the mouth speaketh. A good man out of the good treasure of the heart bringeth forth good things: and an evil man out of the evil treasure bringeth forth evil things" (Matthew 12:34–35). The things of eternal worth are those that cannot be corrupted. They become a part of those whose hearts are changed in Christ.

Blessed art thou, Nephi, for those things which thou hast done; for I have beheld how thou hast with unwearyingness declared the word. . . . I will bless thee forever. I give unto you power that whatsoever ye shall seal on earth shall be sealed in heaven.

HELAMAN 10:4–5, 7

Because he had been a fearless and tireless teacher of the gospel, Nephi was blessed with power and authority. So complete was the trust God had in Nephi that He knew he would not do or say anything contrary to divine will. Because of this assurance, Nephi was granted the promise that all that he asked, all that he said, and all that he did in the name of the Lord would be honored. Nephi would get what he prayed for, because he would not ask for anything amiss. His thoughts and actions were in harmony with the Holy Spirit. God's trust and power come from being valiant in righteousness.

When Nephi had declared unto them the word, behold they did still
harden their hearts. . . . But behold, the power of God was with
him, and they could not take him to cast him into prison, for he was
taken by the Spirit and conveyed away out of the midst of them.
HELAMAN 10:15–16

Transportation by the power of the Spirit to another
place is not without precedent in the scriptures. Nephi,
son of Lehi, attested to heavenly conveyance: "Upon
the wings of his Spirit hath my body been carried away
upon exceedingly high mountains" (2 Nephi 4:25).
Moses was caught up in like manner "into an exceedingly high mountain," where he conversed with God
face to face (Moses 1:1). Similarly, Ezekiel was transported from captivity in Babylon to the temple mount
in Jerusalem (Ezekiel 40:2). The Savior himself was
carried by the Spirit to and from the wilderness of
Judea to the pinnacle of the temple in Jerusalem and
also to "an exceeding high mountain" (JST Matthew
4:8). In the New World, a generation before Jesus'
mortal ministry, the Spirit carried Nephi, son of
Helaman, from congregation to congregation as he
went forth with his divine commission to declare the
word of God unto the people (Helaman 10:17).

O how great is the nothingness of the children of men; yea, even they are less than the dust of the earth. For behold, the dust of the earth moveth hither and thither, to the dividing asunder, at the command of our great and everlasting God.
HELAMAN 12:7–8

Latter-day Saints do not believe in the doctrine of human depravity—that man is born in sin, automatically prone to choose evil, incapable of choosing good, and bent by nature toward personal destruction. Those who choose to chart their own course are indeed captives of their own carnality; they are slaves to their passions and appetites and forever closed to the promptings of the still small voice. Whereas the dust of the earth acknowledges the power of the Almighty and responds to his command, unredeemed man remains less than the dust of the earth through his willful rebellion. We believe in the reality of the Fall, to be sure, and its effects upon us are real. But the Book of Mormon adds the qualifier that those who turn to Christ and put off the natural man become Saints through the atonement of Christ the Lord (Mosiah 3:19). They are thereby redeemed from the Fall.

Therefore, blessed are they who will repent and hearken unto the voice of the Lord their God; for these are they that shall be saved.

HELAMAN 12:23

It has been said that the only two things we do in this life are repent and forgive. Both repentance and forgiveness are soul changes, not mere behavior changes. Faith in the Lord and his atonement are the liberating keys that unlock the prison doors of sin and open our hearts to his healing, redeeming love. Repentance requires self-confrontation, godly sorrow, confession if needed, and humble acceptance of consequences. President Gordon B. Hinckley said, "This is the time, this is the very hour, to repent of any evil in the past, to ask for forgiveness, to stand a little taller, and then go forward with confidence and faith" (*Stand a Little Taller*, 141). Repentance means letting go of heartache and letting the Redeemer in. To be forgiven we must remember our forgiven-ness. Studying the Atonement helps us to acquire a forgiving heart. Pleading prayer can help transform our grieving, angry hearts into soft and forgiving ones. Our progression depends on how we receive these divine gifts.

May God grant, in his great fulness, that men might be brought unto repentance and good works, that they might be restored unto grace for grace, according to their works. And I would that all men might be saved.

HELAMAN 12:24–25

Of Jesus, our exemplar and pattern, a modern revelation attests: "He received not of the fulness [of the glory of the Father] at the first, but received grace for grace" (D&C 93:12). Growing from grace to grace indicates a developmental process, a progression from one level of spiritual attainment to a higher one. "Developing spirituality and attuning ourselves to the highest influences of godliness is not an easy matter," President Howard W. Hunter taught. "It takes time and frequently involves a struggle. It will not happen by chance, but is accomplished only through deliberate effort and by calling upon God and keeping his commandments" (*Ensign,* May 1995, 25). Through repentance, faithfulness, and good works, we are in a position to receive additional attributes and powers of the Spirit through the Lord's divine grace. Growing from grace to grace is the process of a lifetime as we develop and expand the qualities of divinity within us.

*Wo unto this people, because of this time which has arrived, that
ye do cast out the prophets, and do mock them, and cast
stones at them, and do slay them, and do all manner
of iniquity unto them, even as they did of old time.*
HELAMAN 13:24

How do we judge prophets? What are our criteria?
Should prophets be rejected because of their obscurity?
Because they are from Nazareth or Vermont or Salt
Lake City? Because they are little known or because they
have no reputation that precedes them? And what of
familiarity? How many prophets have been rejected
because they had been known for years by the people in
their area? "The trouble with rejection because of personal familiarity with the prophets," President Spencer
W. Kimball explained, "is that the prophets are always
somebody's son or somebody's neighbor. They are chosen from among the people, not transported from
another planet, dramatic as that would be!" (*Ensign,* May
1978, 77). Prophets are men approved of God—what
further and greater recommendation do we need?
Thanks be to the Almighty that he can use imperfect
beings and that these men, molded into vessels of holiness, in time prove a great benefit to their fellow beings.

Behold, your days of probation are past; ye have procrastinated the day of your salvation until it is everlastingly too late, and your destruction is made sure; yea, for ye have sought all the days of your lives . . . for happiness in doing iniquity.
HELAMAN 13:38

This life is a probationary estate, a time of testing, trying, and proving. And like all other tests, it eventually ends. Those who keep their "second estate shall have glory added upon their heads for ever and ever" (Abraham 3:26). But for those who don't, there comes a day of reckoning. When every chance has been given and labor unto salvation can no longer be performed, a judgment must take place. Today, not tomorrow, is the time to prepare to meet God (Alma 34:32–35). Today is the day to forsake evil and seek to be pure before him. It is impossible to find happiness in doing evil (Alma 41:10). We can wear out our lives in efforts to find fulfillment on dead-end, empty streets of pleasure and carnality. But to no avail. Everlasting happiness comes only as we draw close to the Lord, keep his commandments, and strive to become more like him.

*Remember, my brethren, that whosoever perisheth, perisheth
unto himself; and whosoever doeth iniquity, doeth it unto himself;
for behold, ye are free; ye are permitted to act for yourselves;
for behold, God hath given unto you a knowledge
and he hath made you free.*

HELAMAN 14:30

One of our greatest endowments in life is the gift of agency, the power to choose. We are free to choose life or death, good or evil, truth or error (Helaman 14:30–31). Our Heavenly Father will not compel us to be good, and the devil cannot force us to do evil. We are "free forever, knowing good from evil; to act for [our]selves and not to be acted upon" (2 Nephi 2:26). Elder Boyd K. Packer explained, "Latter-day Saints are not obedient because they are compelled to be obedient. They are obedient because they know certain spiritual truths and have decided, as an expression of their own individual agency, to obey the commandments of God. . . . We are not obedient because we are blind, we are obedient because we can see" (*Ensign,* May 1983, 66). Those who see the expanded gospel picture know that obedience to the Lord and his prophets is the key to true freedom.

The people began to harden their hearts . . . and began to depend
upon their own strength and upon their own wisdom,
saying: . . . we know that all these great and marvelous works
cannot come to pass, of which has been spoken.
HELAMAN 16:15–16

Only those who follow the path of true discipleship can know and recognize the works and ways of the Almighty. It is a lifetime pursuit to learn to see the hand of the Lord and to discern the signs of the times. We can be certain that the last thing a sign seeker who demands proof really wants is proof, for once it is given, he does not acknowledge it anyway. Rather, he sees through the limited lenses of his world and thus misses out on the myriad manifestations that come from the hand of him who delights to bless and reassure his children. The cynic quickly provides naturalistic explanations for divine phenomena; he rushes to explain away what believing eyes see clearly is a sign from God. "For what man knoweth the things of a man, save the spirit of man which is in him? even so the things of God knoweth no man except he has the Spirit of God" (JST 1 Corinthians 2:11).

Some were lifted up unto pride and boastings because of their exceedingly great riches, yea, even unto great persecutions. And the people began to be distinguished by ranks, according to their riches and their chances for learning.
3 NEPHI 6:10, 12

Pride is the mother of all sin and the thief of eternal life. While humility would lead one to look up to God, pride leads one to look down upon others. While humility would heighten one's desire to acknowledge the hand of the Lord in all things, pride leads one to rejoice in one's own accomplishments and genius. While humility would motivate one to serve others and dissolve all boundaries and barriers between people, pride would set up petty and pernicious pecking orders in society. The word of the Lord on this matter is clear: "It is not given that one man should possess that which is above another, therefore the world lieth in sin" (D&C 49:20). We can better understand why President Ezra Taft Benson stated that "pride is the universal sin, the great vice" and "the great stumbling block to Zion" (*Ensign,* May 1989, 6–7).

Wo, wo, wo unto this people; wo unto the inhabitants of the whole earth except they shall repent; for the devil laugheth, and his angels rejoice, because of the slain of the fair sons and daughters of my people; and it is because of their iniquity and abominations that they are fallen!

3 NEPHI 9:2

In the midst of thick darkness, the voice of Christ was both felt and heard as a witness and a warning. The destructions that had befallen the Nephites came as a result of their unwillingness to heed the word of the Lord. They had rejected the living prophets he had sent to cry repentance unto them (3 Nephi 9:10). Ruin could have been averted through hearkening to the words of the living prophets (D&C 1:14). The devil laughs when we fall into the traps of pride and disobedience. The only way to avert destruction is by obeying the words of the prophets, the watchmen on the towers who see afar off (D&C 101:45–57). The Lord's arm of mercy is extended toward us, if with full purpose of heart we will come unto him (3 Nephi 9:14). His voice is heard today through the teachings of the prophets and through the whisperings of the Spirit that come to the hearts of faithful followers.

*Ye shall offer for a sacrifice unto me a broken heart and a
contrite spirit. And whoso cometh unto me with a broken
heart and a contrite spirit, him will I baptize with
fire and with the Holy Ghost.*

3 NEPHI 9:20

Christ and his new covenant invite an inner change
of heart that brings about an outward compliance with
commandments and ordinances. Just as ancient ani-
mal sacrifices symbolized the shedding of Christ's
blood and helped the people focus on the Messiah, so
our obedient sacrifice of a broken heart and contrite
spirit centers on our Redeemer. Ours is a living sacrifice that humbly recognizes our dependence upon
Jesus for salvation and a willing submission to him and
his laws (Mosiah 3:19). It means giving away our sins
through faith in Christ and pressing forward with a
steadfastness in him (2 Nephi 31:20; Alma 22:18).
Spiritual rebirth comes because of unwavering faith in
Christ and obedience to his commandments. The
experience of baptism by fire is a continual process,
even if it begins with a singular, dramatic event. Little
by little over a lifetime we move toward godliness.

O ye house of Israel whom I have spared, how oft will I gather you as a hen gathereth her chickens under her wings, if ye will repent and return unto me with full purpose of heart.
3 NEPHI 10:6

The Lord seeks to gather his flock through the covenants of the restored gospel. The promised blessings of his gathering are realized only on conditions of faith, repentance, acceptance of gospel ordinances, and endurance to the end. Each of these demonstrates our willingness to come unto him with "full purpose of heart." The reunion is our free and unfettered choice. He will not coerce us into his protective arms of mercy and love. We must respond to his call and find our place in his bosom. The work of gathering is the fundamental mission of the Church in these last days. To the Prophet Joseph Smith the Lord declared: "For, behold, I will gather them as a hen gathereth her chickens under her wings, if they will not harden their hearts; yea, if they will come, they may, and partake of the waters of life freely" (D&C 10:65–66). A heart full of purpose is a soft, willing, and anxiously engaged heart.

*Behold my Beloved Son, in whom I am well pleased, in whom I
have glorified my name—hear ye him. . . . and behold, they saw a
Man descending out of heaven; and he was clothed in a white
robe; and he came down and stood in the midst of them.*

3 NEPHI 11:7–8

As the people of Nephi gathered around the temple
in the land Bountiful, they heard "a voice as if it came
out of heaven" (3 Nephi 11:3). It was a small voice that
pierced their souls to the center, burning their hearts.
How wonderful that the Father would introduce his
Son and put his divine stamp of approval on Christ's
visit to the New World. How appropriate that the
Savior would come to his temple, minister to the
people, and forever establish in their hearts his gospel
covenant. When the Father has introduced his Son, he
speaks of him as "beloved" and says he is "well
pleased"—a clear example of loving leadership and
perfect empowerment (Matthew 3:17; 17:5; Joseph
Smith–History 1:17). We must likewise hear the heavenly voice and look to God for direction.

I am Jesus Christ, whom the prophets testified shall come into the world. And behold, I am the light and the life of the world; and I have drunk out of that bitter cup which the Father hath given me, and have glorified the Father in taking upon me the sins of the world.

3 NEPHI 11:10–11

After six hundred years of looking forward to the day when Jesus Christ would come and minister to the Nephites, that day arrived. All prophets of all ages have looked to the Savior for salvation. And the faithful have always believed. Now, standing before them in resurrected glory, stood the Light and Life of the world, the One who with pure love worked out the atonement for all mankind. No other could take his place. He alone took upon himself the sins of the world so that we might be saved and find happiness here and everlasting life hereafter. We, like the people of old, cry aloud with one voice, "Hosanna! Blessed be the name of the Most High God!" When we ponder his goodness and glory, we feel to fall down at his feet and worship him (3 Nephi 11:17).

Go down and stand in the water, and in my name shall ye baptize them . . . saying: Having authority given me of Jesus Christ, I baptize you in the name of the Father, and of the Son, and of the Holy Ghost. Amen. And then shall ye immerse them in the water.

3 NEPHI 11:23–26

Nephi was not given additional priesthood power by the Lord, but he was given authority to perform ordinances within the new organization that Christ established among the people. With "old things" done away, Nephi received power and authority directly from the Lord to administer in the "new things." Theirs, like ours, was a dispensation with the fulness of gospel ordinances. The Lord's instructions on baptism were clear and left no room for dispute. He carefully outlined the manner and qualifications for baptism. Much later, when the Church was restored in our dispensation, the Lord again gave explicit instructions to his authorized servants regarding baptism (D&C 20:37, 71–74). The practice of baptism by immersion did not begin in Christ's mortal ministry (Mosiah 18:14–16; Moses 6:64). Its rich symbolism, based on the death, burial, and resurrection of Christ, has been taught from the beginning.

*Verily, verily I say unto you, he that hath the spirit of
contention is not of me, but is of the devil, who is the
father of contention, and he stirreth up the hearts
of men to contend with anger, one with another.*

3 NEPHI 11:29

The Spirit of the Lord will depart where there is
contention, regardless of who is wrong or right. The
adversary's chief weapon is to ensnare us in pride,
which is manifest in the spirit of enmity and strife.
President Ezra Taft Benson said: "A prerequisite condition to increasing faith is to have love and harmony
in the home. Husbands and wives must love and cherish one another. . . . Faults must be overlooked.
Contention must cease. Husbands and wives must be
true and loyal to each other and the sacred covenant
of marriage. Expressions of love must be tendered one
to another. 'Clothe yourselves with the bond of charity,' said the Lord, 'as with a mantle, which is the bond
of perfectness and peace' (D&C 88:125). Yes, love at
home is a prerequisite condition to increasing your
faith" (*Teachings of Ezra Taft Benson,* 527). The antidote for
contention is humility and meekness, and the result is
harmony in our hearts and homes.

This is my doctrine, and it is the doctrine which the Father hath
given unto me; and I bear record of the Father, and the Father
beareth record of me, and the Holy Ghost beareth record
of the Father and me. . . . And whoso believeth in me,
and is baptized, the same shall be saved.

3 NEPHI 11:32–33

The plan of eternal happiness is the plan of God the
Father. The doctrine of the Son is the doctrine of the
Father. The Father and Son bear record of each
other—and of the great plan of happiness. Essential to
this oneness is the Holy Ghost, who testifies of them
both—all so that we can come unto Christ and be
saved. Our Father in Heaven, who is perfectly selfless
and magnanimous, desires that we receive his greatest
gift: the gift of eternal life (D&C 14:7), made available
through God's greatest offering: his Blessed and
Beloved Son (John 3:16). By divine investiture, what
the Son does and teaches is what the Father would do.
What the Father wants is what the Son wants. Their
messenger of peace and testimony, the Holy Ghost,
wants what the Father and Son want. Thus, in one
eternal round of testifying and sustaining, the doctrine
of the Father and the Son rolls forth.

*Yea, blessed are the poor in spirit who come unto me, for theirs is
the kingdom of heaven. And again, blessed are all they that
mourn, for they shall be comforted.*

3 NEPHI 12:3–4

The Savior knows that in this life we will have much
sorrow and heartache, much adversity and affliction.
But we can find comfort, we can find peace and joy, in
the Lord. If we learn to let go of the world and really
let Christ into our lives, we can find "the peace of
God, which passeth all understanding" (Philippians
4:7). Elder Jeffrey R. Holland said, "Some blessings
come soon, some come late, and some don't come
until heaven; but for those who embrace the gospel of
Jesus Christ, they come" (*Ensign,* November 1999, 38).
The key is for us to come unto Christ in all humility
and meekness. If we cast our burdens at his feet and
trust in his tender care, we will feel his comfort. Not
just now but for all eternity, we will feel his everlasting peace.

*Blessed are the meek, for they shall inherit the earth. And blessed
are all they who do hunger and thirst after righteousness,
for they shall be filled with the Holy Ghost. And blessed are the
merciful, for they shall obtain mercy. And blessed are
all the pure in heart, for they shall see God.*

3 NEPHI 12:5–8

The Sermon on the Mount as preserved by
Matthew was given again by Jesus to the Nephites
(compare Matthew 5–7; 3 Nephi 12–14) after the call
of the Nephite Twelve. In this sermon Jesus teaches
the essence of his gospel message: the blessed state of
those who embrace the gospel and strive to become as
he is. The meek, or humbly submissive, are righteous
Saints who live the celestial law and will inherit the
earth when it is sanctified. Those who truly hunger for
righteousness will accept the gospel and be filled not
only with joy and peace but with the Holy Ghost. The
pure in heart are they who possess charity, the essence
of Christian living. In Luke 8:15 we are reminded that
"an honest and good heart, having heard the word,
keep[s] it, and brings[s] forth fruit with patience." If
we desire to draw closer to God, then these virtues
must be our life's study.

I give unto you to be the light of this people. Therefore let your light so shine before this people, that they may see your good works and glorify your Father who is in heaven.

3 NEPHI 12:14, 16

President Gordon B. Hinckley has taught: "Believe in the nature within you, the divine nature, that you are in very deed a son or daughter of the living God. . . . Get above the dirt and the filth of the earth and walk on a higher plane with your heads up, believing in yourselves and in your capacity to act for good in the world and make a difference" (*Stand a Little Taller,* 160). We who have entered a covenant relationship with Christ have both a sacred obligation and blessed opportunity to glorify our Father in Heaven and his Son in thought, word, and deed. The light of love and truth will radiate from all who sincerely strive to overcome the world and follow the Master. As Isaiah reminded us, "Arise, shine; for thy light is come, and the glory of the Lord is risen upon thee" (Isaiah 60:1). The radiance of gospel truth and righteous living can never be dimmed.

If ye shall come unto me, or shall desire to come unto me, and rememberest that thy brother hath aught against thee— Go thy way unto thy brother, and first be reconciled to thy brother, and then come unto me with full purpose of heart, and I will receive you.

3 NEPHI 12:23–24

Jesus encouraged people to resolve their differences (3 Nephi 12:39–42). Most of us realize that if we have unkind feelings toward another person, those unkind feelings need to be dealt with, usually by personal encounter and conversation. But the Master teaches here that if we should discover another has hard feelings toward us, we should go to that person and seek to resolve the matter. The natural tendency on our part is to say, "Wait a minute! That's his problem." Jesus teaches that because we are the object of their discomfort, it is our problem as well. If we have made an earnest effort to resolve issues and soothe the feelings of the other and the individual still refuses to cooperate, then we have done the very best we could do. But that doesn't stop us from praying regularly that their heart would be softened and that the Lord would transform those who had become enemies into our friends (Alma 33:4).

NOVEMBER

*If ye should serve him with all
your whole souls yet ye would be
unprofitable servants.*

MOSIAH 2:21

Behold, it is written by them of old time, that thou shalt not commit adultery; but I say unto you, that whosoever looketh on a woman, to lust after her, hath committed adultery already in his heart.

3 NEPHI 12:27–28

The Sermon at Bountiful is a divine invitation, a call to a higher righteousness, in which Jesus applied a principle called "fencing the Torah." If, for example, a man establishes a personal commandment for himself that he will not partake of alcoholic beverages, then he makes the possibility of keeping that resolve more likely if he avoids walking or driving past the liquor store or the bar. If a person who has been caught up in the web of Internet pornography is seeking to avoid further entanglements, he would do well to avoid using the computer in private. Jesus instructs us that the key to controlling our behavior is to maintain proper control of our thoughts. No one leaps into lecherous behavior without forethought; no one violates temple covenants without planning to do so. If we allow virtue to garnish our thoughts unceasingly, we will be kept from serious sin and will grow confident in the presence of God (D&C 121:45).

*Therefore I would that ye should be perfect even as I,
or your Father who is in heaven is perfect.*

3 NEPHI 12:48

Ultimately, perfection comes as a gift from God to the faithful. A little at a time, as we put off the natural man and seek the things of eternity, we become changed in Christ. We cannot attain perfection on our own. So we go forward, faithfully walking the righteous path. "None of us will become perfect in a day or a month or a year," said President Gordon B. Hinckley. "We will not accomplish it in a lifetime, but we can begin now, starting with our more obvious weaknesses and gradually converting them to strengths. This quest may be a long one; in fact, will be lifelong. It may be fraught with many mistakes, with falling down and getting back up again. But we must not sell ourselves short. We must make a little extra effort. Kneel before God in supplication. He will comfort, sustain, and bless us" (*Stand a Little Taller,* 348). Our eternal quest is to become like the Father and the Son: perfect.

Verily, verily, I say that I would that ye should do alms unto the poor; but take heed that ye do not your alms before men to be seen of them; otherwise ye have no reward of your Father who is in heaven.

3 NEPHI 13:1

We are called upon to do the right things and to do them for the right reason. Giving alms to the poor, praying, and fasting are noble activities, but they are to be done in such a way that the activity does not draw attention to the doer of the deeds. Those who do the right things for the wrong reasons receive what they have desired—the approval of others. The Savior instructs us to do good works that we might glorify not ourselves but our Father who is in heaven (3 Nephi 12:16). Only as our hearts are purified does our service become entirely spontaneous and unpremeditated, and only then do we qualify for an eternal reward. "Therefore, hold up your light that it may shine unto the world. Behold I am the light which ye shall hold up—that which ye have seen me do" (3 Nephi 18:24).

Lay not up for yourselves treasures upon earth,
where moth and rust doth corrupt, and thieves break through and
steal; but lay up for yourselves treasures in heaven, . . .
For where your treasure is, there will your heart be also.
3 NEPHI 13:19–21

Treasures in heaven come to those who earnestly strive to follow the Savior while in this earthly realm. These are they who exercise faith in Christ, repent and forgive, willingly serve others, keep their covenants, follow the prophets, and draw near to God. In the next life we may be surprised to find that those with great mansions and treasures in heaven are those who didn't have much worldly treasure in this life. They may have gone largely unnoticed by the world, but they are known to God. If we would only spend more time on the things of eternity, the things of lasting value and enduring worth, we would find more joy. Just think of what the Lord has in store for those who love him and obey him: eternal life and everlasting happiness.

He looked upon the twelve whom he had chosen, and said unto them: . . . take no thought for your life, what ye shall eat, or what ye shall drink; nor yet for your body, what ye shall put on. Is not the life more than meat, and the body than raiment?

3 NEPHI 13:25

The risen Lord's commission to take no thought for our daily needs or for the future does not really mean that we should not think upon these things or that we should not plan ahead. Rather, the counsel is to avoid being overly anxious or obsessed with how and in what manner we will be cared for. Though this is a specific directive to the Nephite apostles, the principle is true enough for each of us. We should neither become possessed by our possessions nor preoccupied with our nest egg for years to come. We should celebrate the present, feel satisfaction and gratitude for what we have, acknowledge the Lord for his goodness and grace, and pray continually that he will give us sufficient for our needs. We seek first to build up the kingdom of God and establish his righteousness, trusting that in so doing the things of the morrow will take care of themselves (JST Matthew 6:38–39).

*It came to pass that when Jesus had spoken these words he turned
again to the multitude, and did open his mouth unto
them again, saying: Verily, verily, I say unto you,
Judge not, that ye be not judged.*

3 NEPHI 14:1

For decades the Bible scripture quoted most often was John 3:16: "For God so loved the world, that he gave his only begotten Son, that whosoever believeth in him should not perish, but have everlasting life." In recent times, however, this passage has been overtaken in popularity by Matthew 7:1: "Judge not, that ye be not judged." This change bespeaks the rise of an inordinate tolerance, a tendency to ignore absolute values. Yet, some things are just simply wrong. Jesus never intended that we become as shifting sands in matters of morality and decency. We are required every day to make intermediate judgments that concern our involvement with people and events. What we are not in a position to do (because we cannot know people's hearts and do not have sufficient knowledge) is to pronounce final judgments upon our brothers and sisters—to consign this one to heaven or that one to hell. In regard to eternity, God "hath committed all judgment unto the Son" (John 5:22).

Give not that which is holy unto the dogs, neither cast ye your
pearls before swine, lest they trample them under
their feet, and turn again and rend you.
3 NEPHI 14:6

Our ever-sensitive Lord was not labeling people as dogs or swine. Rather, the Master was addressing a divine timetable by which the gospel is to be presented to the children of God. Just as humans usually eat before table scraps are fed to pets, so there is an order to how and under what circumstances the gospel of Jesus Christ is to be presented. Further, there are prerequisites, an order in which the truths of salvation should be delivered, lest they be ignored or misunderstood. We are instructed to deliver the milk of the gospel first before we fill the banquet table with strong meat (1 Corinthians 3:2; Hebrews 5:12; D&C 19:22). "Go ye into the world, saying unto all, Repent, for the kingdom of heaven has come nigh unto you. And the mysteries of the kingdom ye shall keep within yourselves. . . . For the world cannot receive that which ye, yourselves, are not able to bear" (JST Matthew 7:9–11).

Verily I say unto you, that ye are they of whom I said:
Other sheep I have which are not of this fold; them also
I must bring, and they shall hear my voice; and there
shall be one fold, and one shepherd.
3 NEPHI 15:21

Jesus had spoken to his disciples in the Old World of other sheep that he must visit and give the message of salvation (John 10:14–16). The risen Lord had now appeared to one of his larger flocks of sheep, the Nephites (another fold would be the ten lost tribes; 3 Nephi 16:1–2). Christ is the God of all creation and the God of all the earth, and no nation was to be deprived of either his presence or the principles of his gospel. "Know ye not that there are more nations than one? . . . and I bring forth my word unto the children of men, yea, even upon all the nations of the earth? . . . For I command all men, both in the east, and in the west, and in the north, and in the south, and in the islands of the sea, that they shall write the words which I speak unto them" (2 Nephi 29:7, 11).

*He prayed unto the Father, and the things which he prayed
cannot be written. . . . The eye hath never seen, neither
hath the ear heard, before, so great and marvelous things
as we saw and heard Jesus speak unto the Father.*
3 NEPHI 17:15–16

What would it be like to hear the Savior of the
world pray to his Father in heaven? How could words
express such poignant feelings? Mortal language cannot adequately capture the language of the Spirit.
Jesus' prayer was likely at least as much about what was
not said as what was voiced. The communication was
so full of love that the people were overcome with joy.
They didn't just hear the prayer; they felt it. Though
we do not know what the Savior said, we can be
assured that it was a perfect model of prayer. We know
enough of him, his character and goodness, to say with
confidence that his prayer was sincere, humble, and
heartfelt—full of praise and thanksgiving. The Lord's
prayer to his Father is a divine standard we seek to
approach with our own supplications.

Blessed are ye because of your faith. And now behold, my joy is full. And when he had said these words, he wept, and the multitude bare record of it, and he took their little children, one by one, and blessed them, and prayed unto the Father for them.

3 NEPHI 17:20–21

Our Lord knows happiness and sadness, joy and sorrow. Upon looking into the eyes of the faithful, he is moved to tears. Jesus' love for the children is emblematic of his divine compassion for all who choose to be reborn and claim him as their father. His love is the motivating force behind conversion and obedience—the why and the how we can become as little children (Matthew 18:3). The tender mercies and blessings extended by the Savior to the Nephite children reminds us that through the atonement of Jesus Christ we are able to put off the natural man and become as little children (Mosiah 3:19)—literally born again as the spiritual sons and daughters of Jesus Christ (Mosiah 5:7; 27:25). We are to have the simple faith, pure love, and humble devotion of a little child.

*If ye do always remember me ye shall have
my Spirit to be with you.*
3 NEPHI 18:11

Partaking of the sacrament of the Lord's Supper is a renewal of the baptismal covenant. We promise anew to take the name of Christ upon us and remember him more sincerely. That implies motion more than memory, for we thus promise obedience to the Lord and actions of service to our fellowman. In the context of the sacramental covenant, the word *remember* implies following. Fulfilling our covenant with the Lord necessitates keeping his commandments, doing as he would do. To always remember is not just to *think* about him but is to *do* like him. Pondering is also essential to the process. We learn of him, study his teachings, and think deeply about how they apply to our lives. We strive to be like him; we look for opportunities to share gospel light with others. If we truly remember him, the Lord's promise is sure: We will enjoy the constant companionship of the Holy Spirit. He will lead us, guide us, and walk beside us.

I am the light; I have set an example for you.
3 NEPHI 18:16

If we follow Christ, our Great Exemplar, and endure to the end, we will be saved (2 Nephi 31:16). His life provides the perfect example of righteousness, of courage and commitment, of humble submission to the Father's plan. His baptism in Jordan was to fulfill all righteousness and set an example (2 Nephi 31:5–7). Among the Nephites he established his new covenant, taught the gospel, and healed the sick. He prayed for the people and taught them how to pray. He taught his disciples to administer the sacrament and gave them power to confer the Holy Ghost. He said, "This is my gospel; and ye know the things that ye must do in my church; . . . therefore, if ye do these things blessed are ye, for ye shall be lifted up at the last day" (3 Nephi 27:21–22). His life is the only perfect example, the only sure way to salvation.

And whatsoever ye shall ask the Father in my name,
which is right, believing that ye shall receive,
behold it shall be given unto you.
3 NEPHI 18:20

The Saints of the Most High have been instructed to call upon the Father in the name of the Son by the power of the Holy Ghost. If their requests are right—meaning, if they are good (Moroni 7:26), appropriate, and according to the mind and will of him who knows all things from the beginning—they will be granted. Thus, a key to having our petitions answered is gaining "the mind of Christ" (1 Corinthians 2:16) to such an extent that we pray for that for which we ought to pray. "He that asketh in the Spirit asketh according to the will of God; wherefore it is done even as he asketh" (D&C 46:30). Eventually, our desires can be educated and our wisdom enhanced so that we have the same assurance that Nephi, son of Helaman, enjoyed: "All things shall be done unto thee according to thy word, for thou shalt not ask that which is contrary to my will" (Helaman 10:5).

*If ye know that a man is unworthy to eat and drink of my flesh
and blood ye shall forbid him. Nevertheless, ye shall not
cast him out from among you, but ye shall minister
unto him and shall pray for him.*

3 NEPHI 18:29–30

Jesus instructed his Nephite apostles concerning the administration of the sacrament (compare 1 Corinthians 11:23–30). In this instance, he was not speaking to the multitude. Forbidding someone from partaking of the sacrament on grounds of unworthiness is the responsibility of the "judge in Israel," who holds priesthood keys. If members of the congregation are aware of unworthiness, they may discuss it with the appropriate priesthood leader, but it remains his right, through the spirit of discernment, to allow or disallow someone the blessing of the sacrament. We are each to examine ourselves, not others (1 Corinthians 11:28). Partaking of the sacrament unworthily denies one the promised blessings and spiritual renewal associated with worthy participation in that sacred ordinance. Priesthood leaders—and all Saints— should extend greater concern, love, and service to transgressors, pray for them more fervently, and minister to them patiently, "for ye know not but what they will return and repent" (3 Nephi 18:32).

Father, thou hast given them the Holy Ghost because they believe in me; and thou seest that they believe in me because thou hearest them, and they pray unto me; and they pray unto me because I am with them.

3 NEPHI 19:22

Our prayers are to be addressed to the Father in the name of the Son. That is the pattern the Lord has given. While visiting with his American Hebrews, however, the resurrected and glorified Christ encountered a group of disciples who begin to pray unto him. This was clearly an exception to the rule. Elder Bruce R. McConkie wrote: "Jesus was present before them as the symbol of the Father. Seeing him, it was as though they saw the Father; praying to him, it was as though they prayed to the Father. It was a special and unique situation that as far as we know has taken place only once on earth during all the long ages of the Lord's hand-dealings with his children" (*Promised Messiah,* 561). The attitude of the Nephites was one of pure worship and adoration, just as ours will be when the Master returns in glory to begin his millennial reign.

Then shall the remnants, which shall be scattered abroad
upon the face of the earth, be gathered in from the east
and from the west, and from the south and from the north;
and they shall be brought to the knowledge of the
Lord their God, who hath redeemed them.

3 NEPHI 20:13

Although we rejoice today in the phenomenal growth of the restored Church since its organization in 1830, we look with anticipation toward that day in the future when the great gathering of Israel will entail the baptism and conversion of millions upon millions of souls each year. As the spirit of urgency begins to accompany this work even more and as the number of prepared and empowered missionaries is expanded dramatically, then the walls and barriers in hearts and nations will come down. The chosen people of the Lord in all nations will be gathered home to the message of Christ, to his gospel and his doctrine and will enjoy the full blessings of the house of the Lord in holy places. These shall come from the north and the south and the east and the west—from all corners of the earth. They shall gather to the stakes of Zion and to the mountain of the Lord's house.

In that day, for my sake shall the Father work a work, which shall
be a great and a marvelous work among them; and there shall
be among them those who will not believe it. . . .
But behold, . . . I will show unto them that my wisdom
is greater than the cunning of the devil.

3 NEPHI 21:9–10

Who could have imagined on 6 April 1830 that the tiny gathering of Latter-day Saints would eventually expand so that congregations of the faithful would be found in all lands and temples would dot the earth? The marvelous work and a wonder prophesied by Isaiah (Isaiah 29:13–14) is indeed a miraculous miracle. God called upon Joseph Smith to lead the final dispensation through restoring doctrine and priesthoods and powers. Before his martyrdom, the Prophet prepared the Quorum of the Twelve Apostles by bestowing upon them the fulness of the blessings of the priesthood and granting them a perspective that would empower and direct them after his death. One newspaper commented after the martyrdom of the Prophet and the Patriarch on 27 June 1844: "And thus ends Mormonism." No, the work of the Restoration would not be halted by putting to death its testators, for the testament was in place, and sacrifice would bring forth the blessings of heaven.

*And I will execute vengeance and fury upon them,
even as upon the heathen, such as they have not heard.*

3 NEPHI 21:21

We have scarcely begun to appreciate the everlasting worth of the Book of Mormon. It is a supernal witness of the Lord and Savior Jesus Christ, another testament of his divine Sonship and his atoning mission. It is significant enough that its very coming forth is accounted as one of the signs of the times. That is, the appearance of the Book of Mormon will signal that the great work of the Father, the work of the gathering of Israel, has commenced and will continue in uninterrupted and unhampered fashion into and through the Millennium. "And righteousness will I send down out of heaven; and truth will I send forth out of the earth, to bear testimony of mine Only Begotten; his resurrection from the dead; yea, and also the resurrection of all men; and righteousness and truth will I cause to sweep the earth as with a flood to gather out mine elect from the four quarters of the earth" (Moses 7:62).

*A commandment I give unto you that ye search these things
diligently; for great are the words of Isaiah.
And all things that he spake have been and shall be,
even according to the words which he spake.*

3 NEPHI 23:1, 3

It is one thing for a man to recommend that a people
study carefully the words of the Lord and another
thing entirely to have the Lord recommend that the
people study the words of a man. We here gain a
glimpse into the importance of the words of Isaiah
when the risen Lord commanded that we search those
words diligently, "for great are the words of Isaiah."
Although Isaiah addressed many subjects during a
ministry that spanned four decades, his two central
messages find their place in the Book of Mormon
through hundreds of quotations or paraphrasing sum-
maries: the coming of the Messiah and the destiny of
the house of Israel. In a sense, inasmuch as the gathering of Israel comes to pass first and foremost
through gathering to Christ and his gospel, we could
observe that Isaiah had only one central message:
Come unto Christ.

When Jesus had expounded all the scriptures in one, which they had written, he commanded them that they should teach the things which he had expounded unto them.

3 NEPHI 23:14

One can only imagine what it must be like to sit at the feet of the Master Teacher and be instructed in the truths of salvation! In one verse we learn much about how to teach the gospel effectively, for we note that the Savior "expounded all the scriptures in one." A clarifying verse in the New Testament tells us that the resurrected Christ, while walking on the road to Emmaus, drew upon Moses and the prophets and "expounded unto them [the two disciples] in all the scriptures the things concerning himself" (Luke 24:27). That is, he employed all of the scriptures to demonstrate how all things bear witness of him (Moses 6:63). Each of the books within our scriptural canon makes a distinctive contribution to our gospel understanding, but when joined together, they bear a united testimony of the central Character of all holy writ.

*Bring ye all the tithes into the storehouse, that there may be meat
in my house; and prove me now herewith, saith the Lord of Hosts,
if I will not open you the windows of heaven, and pour you out a
blessing that there shall not be room enough to receive it.*

3 NEPHI 24:10

We can never return to God all the bounteous
blessings he has bestowed; we owe so much more than
we can ever repay. But we rob God if we withhold our
tithes and offerings (3 Nephi 24:8). President Gordon
B. Hinckley has said, "The Lord will open the windows of heaven according to our need, and not
according to our greed. . . . The basic purpose for
tithing is to provide the Church with the means
needed to carry on His work. The blessing to the giver
is an ancillary return and that blessing may not be
always in the form of financial or material benefit.
There are many ways in which the Lord can bless us
beyond the riches of the world" (*Stand a Little Taller,* 364).
Tithing is an outward manifestation of an inward willingness to obey the Lord and sustain his Church. We
are to give, honestly and generously, so that the work
of the Lord can continue to roll forth.

*I will send you Elijah the prophet before the coming of the great
and dreadful day of the Lord; and he shall turn the heart of the
fathers to the children, and the heart of the children to their
fathers, lest I come and smite the earth with a curse.*

3 NEPHI 25:5–6

The closing verses of the Old Testament focus upon
the central role of families in the Father's eternal plan.
The ancients understood that Elijah must return in
the last days to restore priesthood keys that would
bind husbands and wives, parents and children, for
eternity. That coming, which took place at Passover on
3 April 1836 in the Kirtland Temple stands as a most
significant moment in the work of restoration. The
Church and all of its organizations and auxiliaries exist
for one reason only: to assist individuals and families
to come unto Christ and be perfected in him.
Through Elijah "the promises made to the fathers"—
the promise of the gospel, the priesthood, eternal life
and the continuation of the family, and the land inheritance (D&C 2; Abraham 2:8–11)—were delivered to
earth once again, all in preparation for the second
coming of the Son of Man.

Verily, verily, I say unto you, this is my gospel.
3 NEPHI 27:21

Latter-day Saints have grown accustomed to hearing, "I know the gospel is true." Many people have a firm conviction that The Church of Jesus Christ of Latter-day Saints is the church and kingdom of God on earth. But what is the gospel? The Lord Jesus delivered to the Nephites one of the clearest and most powerful definitions of the gospel of Jesus Christ: the good news or glad tidings (D&C 76:40) that Christ came into the world, suffered and bled and died on the cross of Calvary, and thus made a substitutionary atonement for all humankind. From God's perspective, the gospel is the Atonement. We appropriate the Atonement through faith in Christ, repentance from sin, baptism by immersion, the laying on of hands for the gift of the Holy Ghost, and enduring faithfully to the end. Jesus was lifted up on the cross that we might be lifted up—glorified and exalted—by our Eternal Father.

Therefore, what manner of men ought ye to be?
Verily I say unto you, even as I am.
3 NEPHI 27:27

Jesus Christ is the sure standard by which we can measure the quality and direction of our lives. President David O. McKay taught: "That man is most truly great who is most Christlike. What you sincerely in your heart think of Christ will determine what you are, will largely determine what your acts will be. . . . By choosing him as our ideal, we create within ourselves a desire to be like him, to have fellowship with him" (*Improvement Era*, June 1951, 408, 478). The full life of the Savior has not been revealed, but we know enough of his amazing life and love to appreciate his abundant heart; we comprehend enough of his glorious character to follow his perfect example; we understand enough of his intimate and infinite atonement to love him with all our soul and sing praises of gratitude to his name. With full purpose of heart, we have as our lifelong quest to seek Jesus and strive to become like him.

There was no contention in the land, because of the love of God
which did dwell in the hearts of the people. . . . and surely there
could not be a happier people among all the people who
had been created by the hand of God.

4 NEPHI 1:15–16

For two hundred years a Zion community was established among the Nephites. There was no envy nor strife nor wickedness of any kind: All were united in love for the Savior, love for each other, and love for the gospel covenant. After six centuries of "ites"—Nephites, Lamanites, Zoramites, Amulonites, etc.—they were now one in heart and soul for a shining moment. Imagine what it must have been like to live during that time. Would we have been converted enough to feel comfortable in their midst? Would we have needed to change something about our character and commitment to be a part of Zion? Love is the key. When there is abiding love in our hearts, our humility and devotion extends not only heavenward but outward to others. Elder David B. Haight said, "Love has no boundary, no limitation of good will" (*Ensign,* November 1982, 11). The love of God dwelling in our hearts produces happiness, peace, oneness, and, ultimately, eternal life.

They had become exceedingly rich, because of their prosperity in Christ. . . . there began to be among them those who were lifted up in pride. . . . and they began to build up churches unto themselves to get gain, and began to deny the true church of Christ.

4 NEPHI 1:23–24, 26

Converted Nephite Christians created a Zion-like society that abounded in love, righteousness, and unselfishness. After two centuries, dissensions, evils, false churches, and persecutions developed—all the result of pride, the great sin and universal vice. Pride leads to envy and animosity. When pride enters our hearts, we experience contention and division. The pride cycle (being proud, then being humbled, then becoming proud again) is a theme throughout the Book of Mormon. The story continues today: People are humble and turn to the Lord, then they prosper and forget God, fall on hard times, and find need for God again. But the Book of Mormon also bears witness of individuals—such as Nephi, Jacob, Alma, Mormon, and others—who rejected the enticements of the world and endured in faithfulness to the end. To find Christ is to be meek and lowly of heart, altogether refusing to ride the Ferris wheel of pride.

I, being fifteen years of age and being somewhat of a sober mind,
therefore I was visited of the Lord, and tasted and
knew of the goodness of Jesus.
MORMON 1:15

Mormon, the author and abridger of the ancient
Nephite record, was an extraordinary man. Entrusted
with the responsibility of the plates and called to lead
the Nephite armies at a tender age, he fully loved his
people despite the gross iniquity and sorrow continually about him. He was a warrior and a Saint, an
unusual mixture of courage and compassion. Mormon
was sober, meaning he was pensive and mature beyond
his years. The things of the Lord were important to
him. He had been visited by the Lord in his youth. He
also saw and knew the three translated Nephites
(Mormon 8:11). Even more significant, he knew the
"goodness of Jesus" by personally experiencing the
blessing of the Atonement—through faith in Christ,
he was born again and filled with the Spirit. This spiritual transformation is the quest of life for each of us
who seek to know "the goodness of Jesus."

*Ye must all stand before the judgment-seat of Christ, yea,
every soul who belongs to the whole human family of Adam;
and ye must stand to be judged of your works,
whether they be good or evil.*

MORMON 3:20

President Harold B. Lee said that we will be judged
on our capacities and efforts. "All you have to worry
about is that you are doing your best in the place
where you are today. . . . There is nothing you can do
about yesterday except repent. That means if you
made mistakes yesterday, don't be making them today.
Don't worry about tomorrow, because you may have
no tomorrows. . . . if you can always witness honestly
that whatever you did, you did to the best of your ability, and next day try improvement on that, when your
life's end comes, of you it can be said in truth, his was
a successful life because he lived to the best that was
in him. . . . all [the Lord] asks is that we do our best;
and that's the measure by which we'll be judged when
that time comes" (*Teachings of Harold B. Lee,* 64–65). The
Lord sees our efforts; he knows our desires.

How can ye stand before the power of God, except ye shall repent and turn from your evil ways? Know ye not that ye are in the hands of God? Know ye not that he hath all power . . . ? Therefore, repent ye, and humble yourselves before him.

MORMON 5:22–24

To all people, in all times and all places, the command is the same: repent and turn from wickedness. Each of us is a child of God, endowed with something of divinity within us. Ultimately, we are in his hands—like the lilies of the field and the sparrows in the skies. All things come from him, move by his power, and owe allegiance to him. We may be prodigals who occasionally wander from the true God, but he ever stands ready to receive us. We need only turn to him with full purpose of heart. It is in total surrender to God that we gain true victory over sinfulness, fleshly susceptibilities, and the pride of the natural man. The Saints of God are to become as children—submissive, meek, humble, patient, full of love, willing to submit to all things (Mosiah 3:19). We cannot stand before the power of God unless we are ready to bow in meekness and lowly submission.

*O ye fair ones, how could ye have rejected that Jesus, who stood
with open arms to receive you! Behold, if ye had not done this,
ye would not have fallen. But behold, ye are fallen,
and I mourn your loss.*

MORMON 6:17–18

In anguish of soul, Mormon's heart swelled with sorrow as he looked upon the thousands of decaying bodies in the aftermath of the final battles between the Nephites and Lamanites. If only they "had repented before this great destruction" had come upon them (Mormon 6:22); if only they had turned from wickedness and humbly accepted the atonement of Jesus Christ. A modern witness, Elder Neal A. Maxwell, stated: "As Jesus begins to have a real place in our lives, we are much less concerned with losing our places in the world. When our minds really catch hold of the significance of Jesus' atonement, the world's hold on us loosens" (*Quote Book*, 175). Jesus Christ is ready to receive us; he stands at the door waiting for us to knock. May we learn from the pitiful plight of the Nephites by hearkening to the Savior's merciful invitation, thereby preparing to stand before the judgment seat of Christ.

DECEMBER

Seek this Jesus of whom the
prophets and apostles have
written, that the grace of God the
Father, and also the Lord Jesus
Christ, and the Holy Ghost,
which beareth record of them, may
be and abide in you forever. Amen.

ETHER 12:41

I would speak somewhat unto the remnant of this people who are
spared, . . . and these are the words which I speak: Know ye
that ye are of the house of Israel. Know ye that ye must
come unto repentance, or ye cannot be saved.

MORMON 7:1–3

It is vital for us to know who we are and Whose we are. Once we really know that we are children of God and that knowledge is rooted in our soul, then we begin to act accordingly. Likewise, it is extremely important for us as descendants of Abraham, Isaac, and Jacob to know of the blessings that are available to us through the covenant. Of all the things the prophet-editor Mormon chose to say in his final message to the people of the last days, he reminded us that we are of the house of Israel and pointed out the need to secure our place in the royal family through coming unto Christ. We of the last days are thus commissioned to "be loyal to the royal" within us, to be faithful and true to our family heritage, and to remain a strong link in the eternal family chain (Lee, "Be Loyal to the Royal within You").

*The Lamanites are at war one with another; and the whole face of
this land is one continual round of murder and bloodshed;
and no one knoweth the end of the war.*

MORMON 8:8

The Book of Mormon is filled with "many seasons
of serious war" (Omni 1:3) because contention and
conflict always follow pride, iniquity, and enmity
(Alma 50:21; Helaman 11:1). "The war goes on," said
President Gordon B. Hinckley. "It is waged across the
world over the issues of agency and compulsion. It is
waged by an army of missionaries over the issues of
truth and error. It is waged in our own lives, day in and
day out, in our homes, in our work, in our school asso-
ciations; it is waged over questions of love and respect,
of loyalty and fidelity, of obedience and integrity. We
are all involved in it. . . . We are winning, and the
future never looked brighter" (*Ensign,* November 1986,
45). The Book of Mormon also speaks of seasons of
peace, periods when charity and uprightness reigned
in the hearts of the people (4 Nephi 1:1–18). Where
there is sin, always there is war. Where there is righteousness, always there is peace.

Behold, I speak unto you as if ye were present, and yet ye are not.
But behold, Jesus Christ hath shown you unto me,
and I know your doing.
MORMON 8:35

Those who have more than a nodding acquaintance with the books within the standard works sense a special spirit associated with the Book of Mormon. Its doctrine and principles and precepts are clear and crisp and penetrating. In addition, the Book of Mormon is the only book within the canon of scripture in which prophet-leaders speak directly to the readers. Moses and Abraham and Isaiah, Jesus and Peter and Paul—these all saw the future and spoke of it. But only in the Book of Mormon do we encounter scriptural passages where the prophet indicates that he sees our day and is speaking directly to us as a result of his vision. Many of the Nephite prophets saw our day—our challenges, obstacles, and the diabolical assault that would face us—and they organized the golden plates to offer warnings, solutions, and encouragement.

God has not ceased to be a God of miracles. Behold, are not the things that God hath wrought marvelous in our eyes? Yea, and who can comprehend the marvelous works of God?

MORMON 9:15–16

Pure rationalists cannot comprehend the majesty of a loving God of miracles, who dispenses revelations as the dew from heaven and pours out gifts upon the faithful. Our unchangeable God responds to our trust and faith (Mormon 9:18–25). Although the process is incomprehensible to finite minds, the faithful know that by the word of God the heaven and the earth were made, by his word man and woman were created, and by the power of his word countless miracles have been wrought (Mormon 9:17). The greatest miracle, however, is the quiet explosion that happens in their hearts as believers respond to the promptings of the Spirit and accept the truth. The mighty change of becoming new creatures in Christ is most miraculous of all. Once lost, now found; once in darkness, now in the marvelous light of truth; once beset by sin, now no longer having a disposition to do evil. This day and always, God continues to work miracles of the heart.

*Condemn me not because of mine imperfection, neither my
father, because of his imperfection, neither them who have
written before him; but rather give thanks unto God that he hath
made manifest unto you our imperfections, that ye may learn to
be more wise than we have been.*

MORMON 9:31

We can learn much from the successes and triumphs of remarkable individuals, but we may learn more from their mistakes, their imperfections and difficulties. The extraordinary authors of the Book of Mormon provide a model. They were human, they had strengths and weaknesses, but, all in all, they did their best, striving with all their heart to put off the natural man, live righteously, and bring others unto the Lord. They, of course, knew heartache and sorrow, conflicts and challenges. Yet rising above their humanness was a strength of soul, a commitment to Christ, and a determination, day by day, to endure in faith to the end. Their sacred record was written for us today. We can be instructed and inspired in its pages, edified and enlightened in its truth. Rejoice and thank God for the supernal gift of this holy book of scripture, written by mortals yet containing the fulness of the everlasting gospel.

*This is a choice land, and whatsoever nation shall possess it shall
be free from bondage, and from captivity, and from all other
nations under heaven, if they will but serve the God of the land,
who is Jesus Christ, who hath been manifested by the
things which we have written.*

ETHER 2:12

God loves all people of all nations and is no
respecter of persons (Acts 10:34). Any home or village
or state or country that chooses righteousness and
submits to the Lordship of Christ becomes a promised
land. The land of America, however, holds a special
place within God's heart, for it was in America that
mortal life began, that the gospel was restored in its
fulness in the last days, and where the center stake of
the New Jerusalem shall be established. There are no
guarantees of preservation for the people of America
except serving the God of the land, who is Jesus
Christ. As long as America remains a truly God-fearing nation, the blessings of God will be felt and
enjoyed by the people of the land, including the blessing of freedom.

*The Lord came again unto the brother of Jared, and stood in a
cloud and talked with him. And for the space of three hours did
the Lord talk with the brother of Jared, and chastened him
because he remembered not to call upon the name of the Lord.*
ETHER 2:14

Sometimes when all is well, when life is reasonably
smooth, we might allow our prayers to become less
fervent, more casual and routine. We might call upon
the Lord in word but not in faith and deed. Or,
because of fear or complacency, we might delay our
pressing forward into an unknown future. The
brother of Jared and his family had enjoyed relative
comfort as they "dwelt in tents upon the seashore for
the space of four years" (Ether 2:13). The Lord had
taught them and prepared them, but it appears that
they had tarried too long, for which the brother of
Jared was chastened. From this account we learn that
calling upon the Lord is much more than merely saying prayers. Calling upon the Lord requires not only
frequency and fervency of prayer but also action—
commitment to do what the Lord commands. The
Lord would have us pray with real intent and, without
delay, act upon his counsels.

The Lord said unto the brother of Jared: What will ye that I should do that ye may have light in your vessels? Therefore what will ye that I should prepare for you that ye may have light when ye are swallowed up in the depths of the sea?
ETHER 2:23, 25

Receiving revelation is often a strenuous endeavor that requires intellectual effort combined with faith and spiritual yearning. The Lord expects us to use our talents, intellect, and common sense as we seek solutions to our problems and answers to our questions. We may approach our prayers the way Oliver Cowdery did when he erroneously assumed that the Lord would grant him his desires merely for the asking (D&C 9:7–8). It may be that when we are praying about our problems and our own unique needs, the Father is saying to us: "What will ye that I should do?" We may forfeit spiritual growth, greater personal revelation, and inspired instructions from the Lord because, expecting the Lord to do all the work, we give no serious study or thought to the solutions but merely ask. The Lord wants us to develop the attributes of godliness; his expectation is that our prayerful petitions will be accompanied by resourcefulness and initiative, by searching and pondering.

Never have I showed myself unto man whom I have created, for never has man believed in me as thou hast. Seest thou that ye are created after mine own image? Yea, even all men were created in the beginning after mine own image.

ETHER 3:15

Although we are not completely certain of the full meaning of this passage, it dramatizes the consummate faith and childlike trust of the brother of Jared. Having acknowledged that Jehovah is a God of truth and having been redeemed from the Fall, the brother of Jared had such faith that he simply could not be kept from within the veil (Ether 3:19; 12:21). The Almighty does not reveal himself to unredeemed man, but he is bound to reward their faith when they come to him in simplicity and purity (D&C 82:10). Perhaps Jehovah was saying, in essence, Never have I revealed myself in such a complete and total manner before now, for never has any man demonstrated such perfect faith in seeking my face.

He saw the finger of Jesus, which, when he saw, he fell with fear;
for he knew that it was the finger of the Lord; and he had faith no
longer, for he knew, nothing doubting. Wherefore, having this
perfect knowledge of God, he could not be kept from within the veil.
ETHER 3:19–20

Faith can be supplanted with perfect understanding and complete confidence in God and his truth, which can take us to the other side of the veil. When we gain perfect knowledge of any particular matter, our faith in that matter becomes dormant. It does not, however, mean we no longer have or need faith. Knowledge and faith are not opposites. God possesses all knowledge and all faith; he has perfect knowledge and perfect faith. A knowledge of all things is part of the faith encompassed in the power of God. It is by virtue of his faith, existing in him in perfection as a principle of power and action, that the worlds were made (Hebrews 11:3; *Lectures on Faith* 1–2). Knowledge and faith are complementary and synergistic—they build upon one another and lead to the desire to attain more of each. If we are humble and teachable, knowledge can lead to greater faith, and faith can lead to greater knowledge.

Good cometh of none save it be of me, . . . and he that will not
believe me will not believe the Father who sent me.
For behold, I am the Father, I am the light,
and the life, and the truth of the world.

ETHER 4:12

The Lord Jehovah taught the brother of Jared that Christ is both the Father and the Son (as much later, Abinadi taught wicked King Noah and his priests; Mosiah 15:1–5). Christ will be called the Father because he was conceived by the power of God and he inherited all of the divine endowments, including immortality, of his exalted Father. He will be called the Son because of his flesh—his mortal inheritance from his mother, Mary. Therefore Christ will be both flesh and spirit, both man and God, both Son and Father. The Father and Son, though separate personages, are one: one in mind, purpose, and glory. All good things come from the light, life, and truth found in them.

Whoso believeth in God might with surety hope for a better world, yea, even a place at the right hand of God, which hope cometh of faith, maketh an anchor to the souls of men, which would make them sure and steadfast, always abounding in good works, being led to glorify God.

ETHER 12:4

On a cold Sunday evening in February 1993 at Brigham Young University, President Howard W. Hunter delivered an exceptional fireside talk entitled "An Anchor to the Souls of Men" (*Ensign*, October 1993, 70–73). This humble and beloved special witness testified: "I promise you in the name of the Lord whose servant I am that God will always protect and care for his people. We will have our difficulties the way every generation and people have had difficulties. . . . But with the gospel of Jesus Christ you have every hope and promise and reassurance. The Lord has power over his Saints and will always prepare places of peace, defense, and safety for his people. When we have faith in God we can hope for a better world—for us personally and for all mankind. . . . Disciples of Christ in every generation are invited, indeed commanded, to be filled with a perfect brightness of hope" (2 Nephi 31:20).

*I give unto men weakness that they may be humble; and my grace
is sufficient for all men that humble themselves before me; for
if they humble themselves before me, and have faith in me,
then will I make weak things become strong unto them.*

ETHER 12:27

The peace and joy that come from conquering the natural man are promised to those who are teachable and humble and who exercise courage and faith. The adversary would have us concede defeat, abandon hope, give in to sin and self-deception, and mislead us to believe that our weaknesses are congenital and cannot be overcome. But our weaknesses can become strengths; our shortcomings can become our strong points. Many struggle with susceptibilities and inclinations that if left unchecked could lead to iniquity and despair. But, thanks be to God, inasmuch as we are humble and faithful and call upon his name continually, the Lord will give us the victory (D&C 104:82). Our weaknesses can make us better or bitter, more humble or antagonistic. As we come unto him, he will help us to see things the way they really are—our faults and foibles, strengths and weakness—so that we can make changes, overcome, and progress as we strive to develop the attributes of godliness.

*Thou hast loved the world, even unto the laying down of thy life
for the world, that thou mightest take it again to prepare a
place for the children of men. And now I know that this love
which thou hast had for the children of men is charity.*

ETHER 12:33–34

Elder Jeffrey R. Holland wrote: "True charity has
been known only once. It is shown perfectly and
purely in Christ's unfailing, ultimate, and atoning love
for us. . . . It is as demonstrated in Christ that 'charity
never faileth.' It is that charity—his pure love for us—
without which we would be nothing, hopeless, of all
men and women most miserable. Truly, those found
possessed of the blessings of his love at the last day—
the Atonement, the Resurrection, eternal life, eternal
promise—surely it shall be well with them" (*Christ and
the New Covenant,* 336). Having experienced the love of
God in our own lives through his forgiveness and his
divine enabling power, we are in a position to reach
out, lift up, and liberate those who struggle with life's
challenges. "Beloved, if God so loved us, we ought also
to love one another. . . . We love him [and our brothers
and sisters], because he first loved us" (1 John 4:11, 19).

I would commend you to seek this Jesus of whom the prophets and apostles have written, that the grace of God the Father, and also the Lord Jesus Christ, and the Holy Ghost, which beareth record of them, may be and abide in you forever. Amen.

ETHER 12:41

In Jesus and in him alone is to be found the abundant life and a fulness of joy (John 10:10; D&C 101:36). In him is the power, the means, whereby through appropriate reconciliation we may resume our status in the royal family of God (John 1:11–12; D&C 34:1–4). If our gaze is upon the Savior, we need pay no attention to the discordant voices around us. His sacred summons is ever before our gaze: "Look unto me in every thought; doubt not, fear not" (D&C 6:36). The grace of God is unmerited favor, unearned divine assistance, the enabling power that we receive from day to day to do what we could never do on our own. Although the greatest of all the gifts of God is free, there is something we must do—we must receive the gift. True faith in the Lord always produces faithfulness. God and his children are at work together in the salvation of the human soul.

After they had been received unto baptism, and were wrought
upon and cleansed by the power of the Holy Ghost, they were
numbered among the people of the church of Christ;
and their names were taken, that they might be remembered
and nourished by the good word of God.

MORONI 6:4

Retention of new converts is always a product of true conversion—of the missionaries as well as the investigators. When the one teaching the gospel is spiritually prepared and the one receiving the message is earnest, humble, and repentant, then both are edified and rejoice together (D&C 50:22). After baptism, new members are numbered among the household of faith. Like tender plants, they must be nurtured wisely if they are to enjoy the spiritual growth and staying power that the Lord desires. They're entitled to a friend, someone to stand beside them, walk with them, and lead them to answers to their questions. They're entitled to an assignment, a calling in the Church, an opportunity to serve in the kingdom of God and bless the lives of others as well as their own. They're entitled to be nurtured by the good word of God, to be taught the gospel in plainness and purity, to be built up in their faith and understanding (Hinckley, Conference Report, October 1997, 71).

*I would speak unto you that are of the church, that are the
peaceable followers of Christ, and that have obtained a sufficient
hope by which ye can enter into the rest of the Lord, from this
time henceforth until ye shall rest with him in heaven.*

MORONI 7:3

A peaceful assurance born of righteousness and
trust in the Lord characterizes true followers of the
Prince of Peace. They enter into God's rest hereafter
because they have experienced God's rest here.
President Joseph F. Smith spoke of God's rest: "It
means entering into the knowledge and love of God,
having faith in his purpose and in his plan, to such an
extent that we know we are right, and that we are not
hunting for something else, we are not disturbed by
every wind of doctrine, or by the cunning and craftiness of men who lie in wait to deceive. . . . I pray that
we may all enter into God's rest—rest from doubt,
from fear, from apprehension of danger, rest from the
religious turmoil of the world" (*Gospel Doctrine,* 58).
Followers of Christ have a sure conviction of the truth
which comes through their hope in Christ and their
faith that he will in time bestow upon them the riches
of eternity.

The Spirit of Christ is given to every man, that he may know good from evil; wherefore, I show unto you the way to judge; for every thing which inviteth to do good, and to persuade to believe in Christ, is sent forth by the power and gift of Christ.

MORONI 7:16

Every person born into this life is given the light of Christ (John 1:9; D&C 84:44–53). One of the functions of the light of Christ is conscience, an inner sense of right and wrong, good and evil. In addition, this light, if heeded, will lead one to believe in Jesus Christ and to accept him as Lord and Savior. One need not be a Latter-day Saint to possess such a witness. Mormon counseled us to broaden our perspective and recognize that God is working through good men and women throughout the earth—not just through Latter-day Saints—to bring to pass his purposes. A modern revelation encourages us to "thank the Lord thy God in all things" (D&C 59:7). In that spirit, we offer up our gratitude to an all-knowing, all-loving God who "doth grant unto all nations, of their own nation and tongue, to teach his word, yea, in wisdom, all that he seeth fit that they should have" (Alma 29:8).

Charity is the pure love of Christ, and it endureth forever;
and whoso is found possessed of it at the last day,
it shall be well with him.

MORONI 7:47

Elder Jeffrey R. Holland wrote: "The charity or 'the pure love of Christ' we are to cherish can be interpreted two ways. One of its meanings is the kind of merciful, forgiving love Christ's disciples should have one for another. That is, all Christians should try to love as the Savior loved, showing pure, redeeming compassion for all. . . . The greater definition of 'the pure love of Christ,' however, is not what we as Christians try but largely fail to demonstrate toward others but rather what Christ totally succeeded in demonstrating toward us" (*Christ and the New Covenant,* 337). His perfect model of loving kindness is the best explanation of what charity is. Pure love comes from a pure source: it comes from heaven.

Pray unto the Father with all the energy of heart, that ye may be filled with this love, which he hath bestowed upon all who are true followers of his Son, Jesus Christ; that ye may become the sons of God.
MORONI 7:48

True followers of the Master pray to be filled with love. "When we understand our relationship to God, we also understand our relationship to one another," said Elder Dallin H. Oaks. "All men and women on this earth are the offspring of God, spirit brothers and sisters. What a powerful idea! No wonder God's Only Begotten Son commanded us to love one another. If only we could do so! What a different world it would be if brotherly and sisterly love and unselfish assistance could transcend all boundaries of nation, creed and color. Such love would not erase all differences of opinion and action, but it would encourage each of us to focus our opposition on actions rather than actors. The eternal truth that our Heavenly Father loves all his children is an immensely powerful idea" (*Ensign,* November 1995, 25). The surest measure of our Christian devotion is our love for God's offspring, our fellowman.

It is solemn mockery before God, that ye should baptize little children. Behold I say unto you that this thing shall ye teach— repentance and baptism unto those who are accountable and capable of committing sin.
MORONI 8:9–10

The light of the restored gospel clarifies that it is incorrect to teach that children are born in sin and, unless baptized, are doomed to eternal damnation. The baptizing of infants evidences a misunderstanding of the atonement of Jesus Christ and the principles and ordinances of his gospel. Those who die without achieving personal accountability (without accountability there is no sin; without sin, there is no need for repentance and baptism) are redeemed by Christ. "Little children are redeemed from the foundation of the world through mine Only Begotten" (D&C 29:46). Little children, like everyone else, are subject to the effects of the Fall (sickness, death, and sin). They are not held accountable for their actions, however. Little children are saved without condition— without faith, repentance, or baptism. Their innocence is affirmed by the tender mercies of an all-loving Lord.

Little children need no repentance, neither baptism. Behold,
baptism is unto repentance to the fulfilling the commandments
unto the remission of sins. But little children are alive in Christ,
even from the foundation of the world.
MORONI 8:11–12

Mormon's epistle on infant baptism is one of the most significant doctrinal discourses in the Book of Mormon, strongly condemning those who teach and practice it. Elder James E. Talmage has written of the sacrilege of infant baptism: "No one having faith in the word of God can look upon the child as culpably wicked; such an innocent being needs no initiation into the fold, for he has never strayed therefrom; he needs no remission of sins for he has committed no sin; and should he die before he has become contaminated by the sins of earth he will be received without baptism into the paradise of God" (*Article of Faith,* 125). Little children are "alive in Christ" because of the Savior's infinite atonement, which redeems them from the effects—both temporal and spiritual—of the fall of Adam. What comfort this sweet doctrine brings: little children are heirs to the celestial kingdom.

*The remission of sins bringeth meekness, and lowliness of heart;
and because of meekness and lowliness of heart cometh the
visitation of the Holy Ghost, which Comforter filleth with hope
and perfect love, which love endureth by diligence
unto prayer, until the end shall come.*

Moroni 8:26

When we feel sorry for what we have done or failed
to do, then our hearts become softened, our spirits are
subdued, and heavenly consolation is forthcoming. We
want to be filled with hope and love; we want to make
things right; we desire with all our hearts to be diligent
in hearkening to the Spirit in resisting wickedness as we
walk the gospel path. When, on the other hand, we
cover our sins with haughtiness and excuses, we stumble
with self-deception and the Spirit withdraws. The door
to everlasting freedom and ultimate happiness is opened
by wholly surrendering to the Lord, by placing everything—our will, our desires—upon God's altar with the
submissive plea, "Thy will be done." The visitation of
the Holy Ghost that fills us with hope and charity comes
to us as disciples of Christ through faith, repentance,
baptism, and continued obedience and steadfastness.
Greater faith, hope, and charity are among the many
fruits of spiritual rebirth and remission of sins.

Notwithstanding their hardness, let us labor diligently; for if we should cease to labor, we should be brought under condemnation; for we have a labor to perform whilst in this tabernacle of clay, that we may conquer the enemy of all righteousness, and rest our souls in the kingdom of God.

MORONI 9:6

No matter how dismal or hopeless the situation may appear in the world, "we have a labor to perform whilst in this tabernacle of clay." We have work to do. We have a message to deliver. We have souls to save. Fully aware that not everyone who hears the message of the restored gospel will receive it enthusiastically, we will take it to all nations nonetheless. Fully aware that there are billions of people who have died without a knowledge of the gospel, we shall continue to labor in holy places in their behalf, one by one. This is an optimism born of faith, an attitude of enduring to the end that will not only bless the lives of those we serve but also empower us to "conquer the enemy of all righteousness, and rest our souls in the kingdom of God."

My son, be faithful in Christ; . . . may Christ lift thee up, and may his sufferings and death, and the showing his body unto our fathers, and his mercy and long-suffering, and the hope of his glory and of eternal life, rest in your mind forever.
MORONI 9:25

Elder Dallin H. Oaks declared: "Jesus Christ is the Only Begotten Son of God the Eternal Father. He is our Creator. He is our Teacher. He is our Savior. His atonement paid for the sin of Adam and won victory over death, assuring resurrection and immortality for all men. He is all of these, but he is more. Jesus Christ is the Savior, whose atoning sacrifice opens the door for us to be cleansed of our personal sins so that we can be readmitted to the presence of God. He is our Redeemer" (*Ensign,* November 1988, 65). Christ lifts us when discouraged, comforts us when heartbroken, extends his encompassing mercy and perfect love, and redeems us from sin and suffering because of his infinite and intimate atonement. Our hope for eternal life and unending joy is in Christ. Of him must we think. To him must we look. Him must we faithfully follow.

*I would exhort you that ye would ask God, the Eternal Father,
in the name of Christ, if these things are not true;
and if ye shall ask with a sincere heart, with real intent,
having faith in Christ, he will manifest the truth of it unto you,
by the power of the Holy Ghost.*

MORONI 10:4

Moroni's promise is perhaps the best known, most frequently quoted scripture in the entire Book of Mormon. It is the closing witness of a prophet of God. The truth of the book rests on his simple, sublime assurance. He thus gives us the key to open the door of light and truth: a sincere heart and real intent. Seldom will a person who approaches the Book of Mormon with a skeptical mind or a desire to prove it false come away with the witness that is delivered by the sweet whisperings of the Spirit to a humble and honest seeker. It is by the power of the Holy Ghost that we know when something is true or not. It is by the power of the Holy Ghost that we can have discernment. If we sincerely seek, humbly ask, and truly desire with all our hearts to know the truth, we will find it within the pages of this sacred scripture.

*Deny not the gifts of God, for they are many; and they come from
the same God. And there are different ways that these
gifts are administered; but it is the same God who
worketh all in all; and they are given by the manifestations
of the Spirit of God unto men.*

MORONI 10:8

The gifts of the Spirit are gifts that always characterize the people of the covenant. Faith is not built upon signs, but signs "follow those that believe" (D&C 63:9). Moroni's caution that we "deny not the power of God" and that we "deny not the gifts of God" may be seen in two ways (Moroni 10:7). The people of the faith should never be found among cynics and doubters who do not acknowledge the place of spiritual gifts or the need for them, and they should also see to it that nothing in their personal lives would deny or block the manifestation of these gifts among them. Every person possesses at least one spiritual gift (D&C 46:11). "Therefore, let every man stand in his own office, and labor in his own calling," for "the body hath need of every member, that all may be edified together, that the system may be kept perfect" (D&C 84:109–10).

Wherefore, there must be faith; and if there must be
faith there must also be hope; and if there must
be hope there must also be charity.
MORONI 10:20

Faith and hope are companion doctrines. Indeed, in some passages of scripture the words seem to be used almost interchangeably. To have faith in Christ is to believe in him, in what he has done, and in what he will yet do for each of us. To have faith is to have complete confidence, total trust, and single-minded reliance upon the merits and mercy of the Master. Hope is not worldly wishing but rather anticipation, expectation, and assurance. Those who have true faith in Christ will have hope in Christ and feel the assurance, born of the Spirit, that they are on course now for eternal life hereafter (Moroni 7:40–42). Out of faith and hope in Christ, charity, the pure love of Christ that Paul identified as the fruit of the Spirit (Galatians 5:22), begins to manifest itself in the life of the believer. Having enjoyed His love, we are able to extend that love to others. Having been given much, we too may give.

I exhort you to remember these things; for the time speedily cometh that ye shall know that I lie not, for ye shall see me at the bar of God; and the Lord God will say unto you: Did I not declare my words unto you . . . ?

MORONI 10:27

The four principal writers of the Book of Mormon had several experiences in common: each saw the Lord Jesus Christ; each was ministered to by angels; each saw our day and offered warnings to us; and each announced that one day he will stand at the judgment bar of God with us and attest to the truthfulness of what he wrote. This latter promise is a sobering one, for it reminds us that the Book of Mormon is not just another book about religion; it *is* religion. The Book of Mormon is not just another doctrinal treatise; it is an invitation, a strong invitation, to come unto Christ and be saved, or to reject him and his gospel at our eternal peril. The Nephite record itself states that people will be judged by their acceptance or nonacceptance of the book (2 Nephi 25:18, 22; compare D&C 20:13). When it comes to the Book of Mormon, salvation itself is at stake.

God shall show unto you, that that which I have written is true.
And again I would exhort you that ye would come unto Christ,
and lay hold upon every good gift, and touch not
the evil gift, nor the unclean thing.

MORONI 10:29–30

Just before Moroni sealed up the sacred record, he bore strong testimony and admonished generations yet unborn to come unto Christ. We are to seek Jesus and strive to become like him. We should, as the apostle Paul advises, covet the best gifts—the gifts of testimony, faith, wisdom, charity, and revelation (1 Corinthians 12:31). We are to seek earnestly the best gifts, acknowledging that these gifts come from God for the benefit and blessing of our fellow children of God (D&C 46:26). We can pray for these gifts and work to develop them as we shun those things wherein no light is found and stay far away from all uncleanness (2 Nephi 18:19–20). Every good gift comes from Christ (Moroni 10:18). These wonderful gifts descend upon the faithful, who look to the Lord in all things and seek his righteousness with full purpose of heart. Spiritual gifts strengthen our faith and build testimony, while blessing those around us.

*Come unto Christ, and be perfected in him, and deny yourselves
of all ungodliness; and if ye shall deny yourselves of all
ungodliness, and love God with all your might, mind
and strength, then is his grace sufficient for you,
that by his grace ye may be perfect in Christ.*

MORONI 10:32

The words *perfect* and *perfected* may strike fear and apprehension into the hearts of even the best of us. To be perfect is to be whole, complete, mature, fully formed, finished, as when Jesus said to those whom he healed, "Thy faith hath made thee whole." We cannot become perfect on our own, but we are made "perfect in Christ," for he is the finisher of our faith (Moroni 6:4). We are finite; he is infinite. We are incomplete; he is complete. We are unfinished; he is finished. When joined by covenant with Christ, we become whole, complete, and finished. Thus in speaking of those who inherit the highest heaven, the revelation declares: "These are they who are just men [and women] made perfect through Jesus the mediator of the new covenant, who wrought out this perfect atonement through the shedding of his own blood" (D&C 76:69).

Sources

Ballard, M. Russell. *Ensign,* November 1999, 63.

Benson, Ezra Taft. Conference Report. October 1986, 3; April 1988, 3.

———. *Ensign,* May 1988, 4; May 1989, 6.

———. "God's Hand in Our Nation's History." *Speeches of the Year, 1976.* Provo, Utah: Brigham Young University Press, 1976.

———. *Teachings of Ezra Taft Benson.* Salt Lake City: Bookcraft, 1988.

———. *A Witness and a Warning.* Salt Lake City: Deseret Book, 1988.

Children's Songbook. Salt Lake City: The Church of Jesus Christ of Latter-day Saints, 1989.

Cowley and Whitney on Doctrine. Compiled by Forace Green. Salt Lake City: Bookcraft, 1963.

Eyring, Henry B. *Ensign,* July 2001, 13.

Faust, James E. *Ensign,* November 1987, 35.

Grant, Heber J. *Gospel Standards.* Salt Lake City: Deseret Book, 1976.

Haight, David B. *Ensign,* November 1982, 11.

Hinckley, Gordon B. Conference Report, October 1997, 71; May 2000, 87.

———. *Ensign,* November 1986, 45; May 2000, 87.

———. *Stand a Little Taller.* Salt Lake City: Deseret Book, 2001.

———. *Teachings of Gordon B. Hinckley.* Salt Lake City: Deseret Book, 1997.

———. *Way to Be! Nine Ways to Be Happy and Make Something of Your Life.* New York: Simon and Schuster, 2002.

Holland, Jeffrey R. *Christ and the New Covenant.* Salt Lake City: Deseret Book, 1997.

———. *Ensign,* November 1999, 38.

Hunter, Howard W. *Ensign,* October 1993, 70; May 1995, 25.

Hymns of The Church of Jesus Christ of Latter-day Saints. Salt Lake City: The Church of Jesus Christ of Latter-day Saints, 1985.

Kimball, Spencer W. *Ensign,* May 1978, 77; May 1979, 5.

Lee, Harold B. "Be Loyal to the Royal within You." *Speeches of the Year, 1973.* Provo, Utah: Brigham Young University Press, 1974.

———. *Teachings of Harold B. Lee.* Compiled by Clyde J. Williams. Salt Lake City: Bookcraft, 1996.

Maxwell, Neal A. *The Neal A. Maxwell Quote Book.* Compiled by Cory H. Maxwell. Salt Lake City: Bookcraft, 1997.

McConkie, Bruce R. *A New Witness for the Articles of Faith.* Salt Lake City: Deseret Book, 1985.

———. *Doctrines of the Restoration.* Compiled by Mark L. McConkie. Salt Lake City: Bookcraft, 1989.

———. *The Promised Messiah.* Salt Lake City: Deseret Book, 1981.

McKay, David O. *Improvement Era,* June 1951, 408; March 1969, 3.

Nibley, Hugh W. *The World and the Prophets.* Volume 3 of *The Collected Works of Hugh Nibley.* Salt Lake City: Deseret Books and F.A.R.M.S., 1987.

Oaks, Dallin H. *Ensign,* November 1988, 65; November 1995, 25.

Packer, Boyd K. *Ensign,* May 1983, 66; November 1986, 17; May 1987, 24.

Proclamation on the Family. *Ensign,* November 1995, 102.

Scott, Richard G. *Ensign,* November 1999, 88.

Smith, Joseph. *History of The Church of Jesus Christ of Latter-day Saints.* Edited by B. H. Roberts. 2d ed. rev. 7 vols. Salt Lake City: The Church of Jesus Christ of Latter-day Saints, 1932–51.

———. *Lectures on Faith.* Compiled by N. B. Lundwall. Salt Lake City: Deseret Book, 1985.

———. *Teachings of the Prophet Joseph Smith.* Selected by Joseph Fielding Smith. Salt Lake City: Deseret Book, 1976.

Smith, Joseph F. *Gospel Doctrine.* 5th ed. Salt Lake City: Deseret Book, 1939.

Talmage, James E. *The Articles of Faith.* 12th ed. Salt Lake City: The Church of Jesus Christ of Latter-day Saints, 1924.

Young, Brigham. *Journal of Discourses.* 26 vols. London: Latter-day Saints' Book Depot, 1854–86. 3:206; 7:289.

ABOUT THE AUTHORS

Lloyd D. Newell and Robert L. Millet are members of the Religious Education faculty at Brigham Young University and authors of *Jesus, the Very Thought of Thee*.

Brother Newell teaches classes at BYU in the department of Church History and Doctrine and in the School of Family Life. He has served as the announcer and a writer for the Mormon Tabernacle Choir broadcast "Music and the Spoken Word" since 1990 and is the author of two books, *The Divine Connection* and *May Peace Be with You*. He and his wife, Karmel H. Newell, are the parents of four children.

Brother Millet is the Richard L. Evans Professor of Religious Understanding at BYU and manager of Outreach and Interfaith Relations with the Public Affairs Department of The Church of Jesus Christ of Latter-day Saints. The author of numerous books, including *Grace Works, I Will Fear No Evil,* and *More Holiness Give Me*, he and his wife, Shauna Sizemore Millet, are the parents of six children.

pg 51 personal revelation